MW00813752

"Insights from the heart of a se
the trenches speaking to the hearts of America's university students

—**Randall Arthur**, Author of *Wisdom Hunter* and *Forgotten Road*

"I have come to truly appreciate the devotionals in *A Word That Sustains.* Ben Gates has a way of capturing a text and helping the reader to discover the treasure of truth and transformation through meaningful illustrations and solid application. What I know is Ben has lived the truth of what he has written, which makes this not simply a good devotional, but one that can bring a depth of perspective and hope to anyone who reads it each day. Read it slowly. Read it prayerfully. Read it expectedly."

—**Ron Williams**, Senior Pastor, Pathway Community Church, Fort Wayne, Indiana

"Every once in a while, God raises up an individual with fresh eyes to see reality from a kingdom perspective. Dr. Ben Gates is such a person. With a strong scholarly background, Ben sifts through the biblical text, connecting the truth with reality in such a personal way that the reader will walk away with a greater view of God. This devotional guide is filled with content and context so that readers will see themselves from God's perspective. They will be encouraged, energized, and empowered to face the world with spirit after having met with God."

—**Reverend Donovan Coley, Sr.**, President/CEO, Fort Wayne Rescue Mission

"If you're looking for something light and easy, this is probably not for you. But if you're looking for food to feed your soul and strengthen your walk with Christ then you will want your copy of *A Word That Sustains.*"

—**Rick Hawks**, Senior Pastor, The Chapel, Fort Wayne, Indiana

"Simplicity, focus, and clarity are gifts in this overwhelming age. Ben Gates delivers these gifts in thoughtful, encouraging, and nourishing bites for the soul."

—**Dr. Randy White**, Author of *Out of Nazareth* and Executive Director, FPU Center for Community Transformation, Fresno, California

"Ben Gates shares insights that remind us of the important things of our journey. He inspires us to face our challenges and changes with the gentle nudgings of the Scripture. His work offers a fresh way to let God's Word take root and give birth to God's Kingdom in our hearts. You will see things differently—guaranteed."

—**Roger Reece**, Executive Director, Associated Churches of Fort Wayne and Allen County, Fort Wayne, Indiana

"Ben insightfully illustrates and applies passages from the Bible, leaving an indelible image on the reader's heart. His anecdotes flow from decades of study and college ministry designed to engage emerging leaders for Christ. You won't want to put it down!"

—**Dr. Mitch Kruse**, author of *Restoration Road*, *Street Smarts from Proverbs*, and *Wisdom for the Road*, and host of the television program and podcast, *The Restoration Road with Mitch Kruse*

"These devotionals are uplifting and empowering. Our ministry has partnered with Ben for over 14 years. We have hosted five teams of students led by Ben. Due to his months of teaching and preparation, the teams were always ready and enthusiastic to serve across all communities in Northern Ireland."

—**Desi** and **Pamela Fisher**, Founders, Adventure Leadership Training, Bangor, Northern Ireland

"Bravo, Ben! Hats off to the sweet evidence that your heart is alive with the One who calls you His own. God has made Himself known to you and in these pages you share the treasures of His heart in perfectly packaged morsels that drive me to His Word. Short, sweet, and meaty, thank you for the feast you prepared for hungry hearts!"

—**Brenda Jank**, Executive Director, Run Hard. Rest Well. Not-For-Profit Ministry

"As Ben's pastor I enjoy the opportunity to be in a Bible study with him. Each week Ben blesses me with his simple, yet profound insights into scripture and life. You will be blessed by those same insights as you read this devotional!"

—**Fred Stayton**, Lead Pastor, Sonrise Church, Fort Wayne, Indiana

"What I love about this book is the mixture of both sacred Scripture and godly wisdom. This is an amazing combination especially when you know the godly wisdom flows from a life of integrity. Knowing Ben personally, I hear his authentic walk with God leap off the pages as my heart is drawn to a steadfast love for the Lord."

—**Chris Norman**, Lead Pastor, Grace Gathering Church, Fort Wayne, Indiana

"Ben Gates makes the Word come alive! In his devotionals he draws you into the biblical setting and makes it relevant for your life. You learn, you feel, you ponder, and you heal. Knowing Ben for many years and seeing his servant heart shared in ministry, it only makes sense for him to use his God-given talents and gifts to continue to bless others in writing. His wisdom to guide people in their spiritual journeys will lead you to a deeper, richer walk with the Lord."

—**Melissa Montana**, CEO/President, STAR Educational Media Network, STAR 88.3

"Ben Gates and I have ministered together over the years on three different continents of the world in a variety of situations, and I know his love for the Lord, his desire to help people grow in their faith, and his commitment to mission. So, reading through these devotions I know they have been borne out of the life of a man who is able to talk the talk because he is walking the walk. Put together Ben's vast experience in Christian leadership, a solid and vital understanding of Scripture, a devoted heart towards God, and a tender heart towards people, and you have a real, dynamic, and anointed devotional resource."

—**Nigel James**, Tour Pastor with the Christian Band Third Day, Cardiff, Wales

# A WORD
## THAT
## SUSTAINS

Rich and Shelley,
your friendship and
support over the years
has meant so much. Hope this
book encourages you. May the
Lord's Word sustain you
as His Spirit leads you.
God bless,
Ben Aston
PSALM 119:105

BEN GATES

# A WORD
# THAT
# SUSTAINS

*40* *Reflections for Today*

*A Word That Sustains*
Copyright © 2021 by Ben Gates
All rights reserved.

Published in the United States by Credo House Publishers, a division of Credo Communications, LLC, Grand Rapids, Michigan credohousepublishers.com

Unless otherwise noted, Scripture quotations are from the Holy Bible, New International Version®, NIV® Copyright ©1973, 1978, 1984, 2011 by Biblica, Inc.®. Used by permission. All rights reserved worldwide.

ISBN: 978-1-62586-187-0

Cover and interior design by Frank Gutbrod
Cover photo by Johann Siemens/Unsplash.com
Editing by Donna Huisjen

*Printed in the United States of America*

First edition

# CONTENTS

*For Jesus and for Janet,*
*My Giver and His gift.*

# PREFACE

Words frame the meaning of life.

At least that's the way it has been for me most of my life. I've always been fascinated with words as far back as I can remember. Trips to the library when I was a small boy to get books full of words that opened new worlds to me. Countless hours spent spelling them as my mother prepared me for middle school competitions, times that built a special relationship for me with her around those words. Crafting speeches with just the right words for high school debate contests—learning to argue just a little bit too well!

Then I met Him. The Word. And that changed everything for me.

Suddenly I learned that words can be used to tell others the difference Jesus has made in my life. What I write or what I say can encourage and strengthen someone when they need a little help just to hang in there for one more day. Why? Because they won't really be my words, after all; they will be His. The prophet Isaiah said it best: "The Sovereign LORD has given me a well-instructed tongue, to know the word that sustains the weary. He wakens me morning by morning, wakens my ear to listen like one being instructed" (Isaiah 50:4). I want so much for my words to be the ones He gives me—for myself, for the ones I love, for those I meet every day.

So, when I became a campus pastor 23 years ago, I decided that I would write a weekly devotion, writing about something in God's Word each week for my students, university faculty and staff, and the friends of our ministry. I called these devotions the "Spiritual Cyber-Vitamin" because I hoped the words about the Word would energize and invigorate the faith of those who read them. This book is a collection of some of those words. I hope they will encourage you.

One thing I know for sure: Jesus is the Word, and that Word does more than frame the meaning of life; He is the Life, the Life that we all desperately need.

# THE MYSTERY AND THE MARVEL OF HIM

# WHERE ELSE CAN WE GO?

*Simon Peter answered him, "Lord, to whom shall we go?*
*You have the words of eternal life."*

JOHN 6:68

One day, Jesus was speaking to a group of people and compared Himself to the manna that God had given to the Israelites during their time of wandering in the wilderness after their exodus from Egypt. During this discourse, Jesus boldly and directly called Himself the "bread of life" (John 6:35). The logical response to this announcement would be to come to Jesus for nourishment and that is the invitation our Savior was extending to His hearers. Jesus dropped all decorum in verse 53 and told His disciples that they must "eat the flesh of the Son of Man and drink his blood" or they would have no life in them. John explains that Jesus was in the synagogue in Capernaum (a favorite teaching spot for our Lord) when He made this controversial command.

The metaphor that Jesus was using here was clearly open to misinterpretation and some of His hearers did not understand what Jesus was asking of them. To the literal-minded, it sounded as though Jesus was encouraging cannibalism; ironically, the Romans thought that early Christians were flesh-eaters because of this teaching about the Lord's Supper. John tells us that many of the disciples called Jesus's words a "hard teaching" and asked the question, "Who can accept it?" (verse 60). Verse 66 explains that many of Jesus's disciples turned back at this point and no longer followed Him. It should be sobering to all of us to realize that disciples, not the skeptical, were the ones who walked away. Jesus then turned to the Twelve and asked them a crucial question: "You do not want to leave too, do you?" (verse 67). Peter's response to this question is recorded at the beginning of this devotion.

The finality of what Peter was saying is worthy of our reflection. It is as though he were saying, "Lord, we often don't understand You or what You are saying to us. It is hard at times to follow You and face the misunderstanding, and even the stigma, that come with being Your disciple. But, at the end of the day, where else can we go? You alone provide the ultimate purpose and meaning to life. There is nothing else and no one else who can replace You in our lives." I believe we all want to arrive at the point that Peter is describing, the point at which nothing in this life and no one in this life can offer me the fulfillment and the significance that come through a relationship with Jesus Christ. The truth is that we all try to find satisfaction and meaning elsewhere—in our careers, our earthly relationships, pleasurable escapes, our technological devices, worldly power or wealth—and so it goes. But Peter was saying that none of this can replace a life with Jesus. Everything else ends in death; only Jesus offers us true life forever.

## P R A Y E R

*Heavenly Father, truly there is nowhere else we can turn but to You. You have the words of life; Your Presence is what brings sense and significance to my existence. Bring me to the end of myself, and help me to realize this so that I don't seek temporary solutions or satisfactions apart from You. I don't want any escapes that take me away from a relationship with You. Allow my life to witness to others that only in You can I truly experience life to its fullest as You intended it to be for me. In Jesus's name, amen.*

# PRAISING GOD FOR WHAT WE DON'T UNDERSTAND

*The secret things belong to the LORD our God,*
*but the things revealed belong to us and to our children forever,*
*that we may follow all the words of this law.*

DEUTERONOMY 29:29

Sometimes I laugh to myself when I hear someone say, "When I get to heaven, the first thing I am going to do is ask God to explain . . . *fill in the blank* . . . to me." I don't think so. I believe that the first thing we will do will be to fall on our faces in adoration and worship in the Presence of the One Who made us, loved us, died for us, and rescued us. I think that any lingering questions will be driven from our minds. Asking God our "whys" here on earth is not particularly fruitful either. Am I the only one who has noticed how inscrutable the will and the ways of our Lord can be? I don't think our questions annoy God, but sometimes they just don't get answered. That's why the verse quoted at the beginning of this selection is so significant. Moses makes it clear that, in this life, there are going to be things that we just don't understand. There are "secret things" that belong to the Lord alone—things that would overwhelm us if we knew them, things that we cannot handle as creatures (as opposed to the Creator), things so mysterious that the truth of them would be lost on limited, sinful beings like us. And that is okay—it should be that way. But there are also things that God has revealed to us, in His Word and through His Spirit, that belong to us and our descendants as treasured spiritual possessions forever. These are truths we have not acquired through human reason or earthly wisdom, but truths we know only because God has shown them to us. The last phrase of the verse makes it clear that what God has revealed to us must be obeyed. God's revelation is timeless, for us and for later generations, to revere, to respect, and to follow.

Through the Old Testament prophet Isaiah, God told us very clearly and directly that our thoughts are not His thoughts and our ways are not His ways (Isaiah 55:8). Rather than provoking frustration, that reality ought to produce praise and worship in our hearts. It simply means that God is bigger than us and our puny ability to make sense of life. I want a God Who is so wise, powerful, majestic, and mysterious that He doesn't fit into any neat little explanation that I might construct for His will and ways. The apostle Paul felt the same way. In his letter to the Ephesians, Paul glorified God precisely because He is able to do immeasurably more than we can possibly imagine (3:20). If He had no secrets from me, He wouldn't be much of a God. Since the secret things belong to God, I am forced to trust Him and His character. And that is the whole point of life in the first place, isn't it? Because He is God and I am not, I have to learn to rely upon His love and provision even when I have no clue what the Lord is up to. In our prayers this week, let's praise God for what He is doing around us that we don't understand or that we cannot see. Small children delight in surprises and who doesn't love a good mystery?

## PRAYER

*Heavenly Father, thank You that You are way bigger than any god we could create or contrive! You are the only God Who is powerful and loving enough to meet our needs. Give us grace to live with the questions as our trust grows daily in Your incomprehensible love and care for us. In Jesus's name, amen.*

# AN EXTRAORDINARY GOD
# ON ORDINARY DAYS

*As they were coming down the mountain,*
*Jesus instructed them.*
MATTHEW 17:9

O ne of the dangers of reading about individuals whose stories are recorded in the Bible is that we can fall into the trap of believing that, somehow, they were more "spiritual" than we are or that their lives were more exceptional than ours. I think they would be dismayed to discover that we feel that way about them, and I know that the Lord does not want us to idolize them. It is important to remember that the Scripture relates the experiences of ordinary people who encountered an extraordinary God in the course of routine, mundane days of their lives.

Think about it this way. Moses stumbled upon the burning bush and the holy presence of the Lord during an average day of tending his sheep (Exodus 3:1–2). The apostle Paul's life was forever changed by an encounter with Jesus while he was traveling down one more lonely road on the way to another city not unlike all of the ones he had visited before (Acts 9:3–9). A blind beggar outside of the city of Jericho sat along the roadside, as he always did, not realizing that a momentous meeting with Jesus was about to restore his sight (Mark 10:46–52). A Samaritan woman went to a well to draw water, as she did every day, not realizing that she was about to meet Jesus that afternoon. She would taste the living water He had to offer for the first time that day (John 4:4–15). Gideon was hiding in a wine press, threshing wheat, minding his own business, when an angel of the Lord appeared to him (Judges 6:11–12). You get the idea. Most of the time, the Lord meets us in the ordinary moments on the average days when we least expect an encounter.

We all love the mountaintop experiences when we feel the exhilaration of a powerful revelation of God's loving presence. But we can't live there. And sometimes those mountaintop "highs" lead us to minimize the significance of the daily grind, when nothing special seems to be happening in our lives and no one seems to notice that we are trying our hardest to follow Jesus faithfully. Jesus told Peter as much when this impetuous disciple suggested that they build shelters on the Mount of Transfiguration. Notice that Jesus led them back down the mountain and told them not to tell anyone about that experience until after His resurrection (Matthew 17:1–9). The work of serving the Lord and ministering to His people is done in the valley, not on the mountaintop—a reality the disciples discovered only too well right after they had descended with Jesus in this instance. In fact, if we measure life based on mountaintop feelings, we will spend endless days disappointed, fearing that the Lord is nowhere to be found. And we will miss the Presence of the Lord in our everyday lives in the process.

So, what is the point of those rare times when God's majesty is seen so clearly and feelings of His presence are so strong? The value of the vision and its accompanying glory is its gift of inspiring us for service and endurance on most of the regular days of our lives. Chances are this week will be filled with the regular and the mundane for each of us. We might be tempted to even feel as though we are running in the same old rut. Yet we need to be aware that Jesus might be just around the corner toward which we are headed. He is the God of gracious surprises, filling routine moments with incredible splendor. Let's be watching for Him to show up when we least expect it.

## PRAYER

*Heavenly Father, we do love the feelings of those mountaintop moments with You. Yet Your work, most of the time, is done in less exalted places at less spectacular times. As Paul wrote Timothy, help us to be prepared "in season and out of season" to serve You (2 Timothy 4:2). Give us patience, endurance, and discipline to trust You and to minister in Your name even when we don't feel as though we want to or are able to. Would You speak to us and meet us during the ordinary days of this week? When You do, those days won't be ordinary any longer—they'll be very sacred and very beautiful! In Jesus's name, amen.*

# THE LORD WHO HEALS

*"I am the LORD, who heals you."*
EXODUS 15:26

Have you ever had one of those days or weeks when you witnessed the power of God or experienced a moment of spiritual victory when you felt the Lord really was with you? And then, almost immediately afterward, something happened that made you question the love of God or His concern for you or your loved ones? That was the sequence of events in the Old Testament book of Exodus, chapters 12 through 15. The Israelites were liberated miraculously by the power of God through the Red Sea from their slavery in Egypt. Now, just a few days later, the people of God were wandering around the desert without any water. They became embittered by their misfortune and began to grumble against the very God, and his servant Moses, who had delivered them from their captivity. Finally, the children of Israel arrived at a place called Marah, but the water there was too bitter to drink—so the grumbling intensified (Exodus 15:24).

What to do with bitterness and grumbling? Throw wood at it! But not just any wood—the wood the Lord showed Moses (Exodus 15:25). And what is the wood that the Lord has shown all of those who trust Him for salvation? The remedy for bitterness in our souls and complaining in our hearts is to cling to the wood of the cross of Jesus Christ. There is a sweetness and a joy that flows out of the self-sacrifice of the Cross. Not only does the power released by the Cross wipe away our sins, but it also transforms our hearts so that we can humbly be thankful in even the most difficult of circumstances—if we keep our eyes fixed on the Cross. If we focus instead on ourselves, we can be overwhelmed by self-pity, anxiety, and discouragement. At the end of the day, our lives can't be about us. We must be about our Father's business and in the service of others. That is the spirit of the Cross and that is the antidote to any bitter taste in our mouths.

Once the water was "healed" and the Israelites were able to drink it, the Lord offered instructions to be followed, a test of the good faith of the people of God going forward. Simply put, the Lord told the children of Israel that if they would listen to what He said and obey His commands, they would enjoy good health (Exodus 15:26). Is the Lord arrogantly demanding obedience, in the absence of which He will make us ill? Is He offering rigid, legalistic believers an opportunity to indict the sick over some unconfessed sin? (Sadly, I have seen some uncaring Christians do the latter.) I don't think so. Most illness is simply symptomatic of the fact that we live in a broken world (ruined by the sin of humankind), where health is one of many casualties. Rather, I think the Lord is saying the following to the Israelites and everyone since that time who has read this account in Exodus 15: "I made you. I know what is best for you emotionally, mentally, physically, and spiritually. My Word is the operator's manual for your life. If you live according to My guidelines, as laid out in the Scripture, you will live a holy, whole, and healthy life."

The Lord's healing can be a mysterious affair. If the Lord is a God who heals, then why don't all people who pray in faith for themselves or for a loved one who is sick experience healing? I don't know. And beware of anyone who tells you they do know why. God in His sovereignty chooses to heal some people instantly and some people gradually and some people not at all on this side of the grave. God chooses to heal some people miraculously and some people medically—and in various combinations of the two. But God does heal all of those who look to Him as Lord and Savior—because He is taking us all home to a place where there is no brokenness, no sin, no disease, and no death. Significantly, the story in Exodus 15 ends with the children of Israel resting after their ordeal at an oasis of 12 springs and 70 palm trees called Elim. This ending is an example of how the Lord will bring us to a place of peace and rest after a struggle or trial that might even be of our own making. The Lord knows just how much we can handle (although we might think He has left us in the storm too long) and will bring us to a place of shelter and stillness just when we need to be there.

## P R A Y E R

*Heavenly Father, thank You that You are the One and only Healer! Keep us from an embittered spirit and an accusing heart. Help us to live our lives in the healthy way You have designed us to live. Remind us to pray to You for the sick this coming week. Thank You that the Bible tells us that the stripes Jesus bore and the blood that He shed on the Cross ensure our ultimate healing. In His holy name we pray, amen.*

# EVEN IF . . .

*"The God we serve is able to deliver us."*

DANIEL 3:17

In the book of Daniel, we meet four young Jewish men who were taken as captives to Babylon to serve in the royal court. Daniel, Meshach, Shadrach, and Abednego decide to remain true to the Lord, His will, and His ways in this alien, pagan environment no matter what the cost. As you read this Old Testament book, you learn that the cost is extremely high at times. In Daniel 3, some of the Babylonian astrologers, no doubt out of jealousy and spite, accused Daniel's three friends of failing to worship a statue of King Nebuchadnezzar whenever a certain musical invitation was played. Shadrach, Meshach, and Abednego were charged with showing no respect for the power of the king and no devotion to his gods in worship.

King Nebuchadnezzar was furious with the young men and summoned them into his presence. The Babylonian king sought to intimidate and lord his authority over the young Jewish boys. Nebuchadnezzar delivered an ultimatum on the spot: "The music will be played and you will bow down, or else . . . you will be burned to death in a fiery furnace." As though to taunt the young men, Nebuchadnezzar asked rhetorically, "Then what god will be able to rescue you from my hand?" (3:15). Shadrach, Meshach, and Abednego responded with a boldness born of the Spirit and of their intimate relationship with their Lord: "King Nebuchadnezzar, we do not need to defend ourselves before you in this matter. If we are thrown into the blazing furnace, the God we serve is able to deliver us from it, and he will deliver us from Your Majesty's hand. But even if he does not, we want you to know, Your Majesty, that we will not serve your gods or worship the image of gold you have set up" (3:16–18). The Lord answered the question posed by King Nebuchadnezzar—He ultimately saved the young men from a fiery death. Indeed, not even a hair on their head was singed by the inferno into which they were thrown.

Those of us who serve the Lord and enjoy a relationship with Him never need to defend ourselves. If we have remained faithful to Him and stand blameless before Him, the Lord will defend us from those who might attack us, criticize us, or lie about us. A lot of times, we bear culpability in our own failures or adversity. But even in those situations, as long as we are humbly repentant and recognize with true remorse our own responsibility in the situation, we can trust the Lord to forgive us, to come to our aid, and to protect us. A lot of times, when we are acting overly defensive, it is a sign that we have not recognized our role in our failure or we are not trusting the Lord to intervene on our behalf.

Notice, too, that the young men testified that the Lord "is able to deliver" and that "he will deliver us from [your] hand." Sometimes, we as Jesus followers confuse His ability to save us with the belief that we know exactly how He will save us. The ways of the Lord are inscrutable. Why does one person with cancer get healed miraculously and another, of similar faith and with just as many people praying for him or her, does not? I fear that at times we venerate a particular outcome to our trials as our god rather than worshiping the Lord Himself. Then, when life doesn't go the way we think it should, we get bitter and charge God as faithless and unloving. Shadrach, Meshach, and Abednego offer the corrective for us in their words. There is no doubt of two things: the Lord has the ability to save us, no question, and He will rescue us, either in this life or, ultimately, in the next. But we must never make the answer to a prayer more important than our relationship with and devotion to the Lord.

Shadrach, Meshach, and Abednego made it clear that they understood the difference between devotion to the Lord under any circumstances and devotion only when life goes the way we as individuals want it to. My favorite two words of all those spoken by these three brave young men are "even if." Even if the Lord doesn't save us from death; even if the Lord doesn't do what we want, expect, or hope for, we will remain steadfastly committed to the Lord. The Lord is our God, not anything in this life on earth. As the Old Testament prophet Habakkuk declared, "Though the fig tree does not bud and there are no grapes on the vines, though the olive crop fails and the fields produce no food, though there are no sheep in the pen and no cattle in the stalls, yet I will rejoice in the LORD, I will be joyful in God my Savior" (Habakkuk 3:17–18).

## PRAYER

*Heavenly Father, we believe that You are able to save us from any problem or predicament. We believe that You will rescue us because You love us more than we can possibly imagine. Thank You for encouraging those who have gone before us and steadfastly modeled for us incredible devotion to You. We want to be people You use to inspire others to remain faithful to You to the end. Help us to lead "Even If . . ." lives—to demonstrate otherworldly trust that amazes the world and glorifies You. In Jesus's name, amen.*

# THE PROBLEM
## AND THE PROMISE
### OF ME

# ME OR HIM?

*"He must become greater; I must become less."*

JOHN 3:30

There are some fairly basic issues when it comes to following Jesus. While I believe that a life of faith can be very profound, I wouldn't say that, at its core, it is very complex or complicated. One of the foundational principles of Christianity boils down to a battle—a battle between self and the Lord. The point of the warfare is the determination of who will be in charge: me or God. This is the basic, twofold question facing all of humankind—Do I believe there is a God, and, if so, will I submit my will to His? The battle began in the Garden of Eden and the warfare continues to swirl around every human heart to this day. The human being who refuses to submit to God will attempt to control his own life, to meet her own needs in a manner consistent with this self-oriented, self-ordered, self-promoted point of view. This person will seek in other places the peace, the love, the strength, the purpose, and the life that only God can provide—and ultimately the frustration and disappointment they experience in the pursuit either leads them to God or away from Him to a hell of futility, bitterness, and despair.

Human glory is the result of being considered better, faster, more beautiful, more powerful, or more successful than others. The glory of self is the result of being favorably *compared* to other people. The better our scores on the scoreboard of life—the more glory we receive. And this glory comes with upward mobility. The higher we climb, the more glory we collect for ourselves. But this same glory also contributes to the darkness of the human condition.

Even our *motivation* to serve must be love for God, not love for our own glory or, more selflessly, for the glory of humanity. If we are motivated to serve out of a love for humanity, we will be defeated and brokenhearted since we will face indifference along the way. On the other hand, if we are motivated to serve by a love for God, no amount of ingratitude from other people will be able to hinder us from serving one another.

At our core, we are all selfish people. We want to put ourselves first—to essentially *be* god. Satan put it in the heads of our ancestors in the Garden that they could "be like gods." We want to be our own masters—as though we have created ourselves and can invent some happiness for ourselves outside of God, apart from God. The sad story of human history—poverty, ambition, war, slavery, immorality—is the long, terrible story of humankind trying to find something other than God that will bring happiness.

How do we turn the tide of battle toward God and away from ourselves? If we want to see and receive God's glory and approval, we need to choose the path of humiliation. God's glory is revealed through *compassion*, not *competition*. More specifically, God's glory was revealed through suffering motivated by compassion for human beings mired in their own selfish sin. In other words, God chose the way of downward mobility—the opposite of human ego seeking upward mobility. If we want to see the glory of God, we must move downward with Jesus—even to the point of the suffering that comes with self-denial and sacrificial service. This is the deepest reason for living in solidarity with the poor, the oppressed, and the marginalized of society. They show us the way to God—the way downward in humility and compassion.

## P R A Y E R

*Heavenly Father, we confess that we can be selfish people. And we can also be self-deceived—thinking that we aren't as selfish as we really are. Mercifully show us the places in our lives where we are still trying to call the shots. Help us to give up trying to be God in those places and allow You to have full control of our hearts. We want to serve You and others with compassion and humility. We want others to see You in our service, not engage in vain attempts at self-promotion. Today, take over our lives and love through us—even in spite of us at times. In Jesus's name, amen.*

# HE IS GOD AND I AM NOT

*Jesus answered, "You would have no power over me*
*if it were not given to you from above."*
JOHN 19:11

Memorable speeches, songs, poems, and letters often have a single line that stands out and creates a lasting impression. This line speaks for itself, and, after hearing it, all present recognize that an important truth has been declared. In our culture, the utterance of such a line would be called a "drop the mic" moment; in the past, someone might have followed such a truth with the comment, "'Nuff said!"

The setting for the powerful utterance that begins this devotion is the trial of Jesus before the Roman governor Pontius Pilate, during which the earthly fate of our Savior was being determined. In what could only be described as a panicked attempt to save Jesus from a Jewish lynch mob, Pilate asks our Lord, "Don't you realize I have power either to free you or to crucify you?" Jesus's response, above, contradicts Pilate's threat with breathtaking clarity and decisiveness.

Jesus's reply to Pilate was the ultimate declaration of independence and freedom. Essentially, Jesus was telling Pilate that He, Jesus, was a very dangerous man; Jesus was dangerous because He had already given up His life and any leverage that Pilate thought he could wield was purely an illusion. And the leverage was not the only illusion here. Whatever political power this Roman governor thought he had was puny, a leaf blowing in the wind compared to the power of Father God to orchestrate His will in the course of human history.

Let's unpack these two powerful truths and apply them to our own lives of faith. First, if I am willing to see myself as dead to the world and alive in Christ right now, then there is nothing the world can threaten or entice me with that will tempt or deter me from obeying the Lord's will for my life. That posture makes a person extremely dangerous because he or she cannot be controlled by the world, the flesh, or the devil—such a Jesus follower is a wild card in the eyes of those who simply do not understand what it means to love Jesus beyond life itself. Jesus called His children to live such a life when He said: "For whoever wants to save their life will lose it, but whoever loses their life for me will save it" (Luke 9:24). The world rarely sees the incredible and revolutionary power of a life given over entirely to Jesus. May the Lord bring each of us closer to this position of abandonment that will allow us to serve Jesus with liberty and without hesitation even in the most life-threatening circumstances. If we will simply realize that we are on our way home to be with our Father and that this life has nothing to offer, by comparison, that is nearly as beautiful and fulfilling as the destination to which we are headed, the decision to live in freedom won't be that hard to make.

The other truth that is apparent in this story is that earthly power is very deceptive and has a seductive capacity to convince those who have it that they are more important than they really are. The arrogance and self-importance displayed by this group of people is almost laughable at times. The psalmist says as much: "The kings of the earth rise up and the rulers band together against the Lᴏʀᴅ and against his anointed . . . The One enthroned in heaven laughs; the Lord scoffs at them" (Psalm 2:2, 4). There will come that startling moment to all of us when we realize that, simply put, He is God and we are not. The Lord offers startling clarity in Psalm 46:10: "Be still, and know that I am God."

P R A Y E R

---

*Heavenly Father, help us to live freely in You. We don't want anything in our lives to compromise our heart's desire to obey You to the fullest extent possible. We know that this sort of life is the life of liberty that we want to experience. Keep us from overestimating our importance, power, or control in this life. We can rest in You because You are in control and Your power overrules anyone or anything that could ever separate us from Your love (Romans 8:38–39). In Jesus's name, amen.*

# HE KNOWS WHOM HE IS MAKING ME TO BE

*Jesus looked at him and said, "You are Simon son of John. You will be called Cephas."*

JOHN 1:42

Each new academic semester at my university brings energy and excitement, but it can also bring apprehension, fears, and even loneliness for young people who may have moved away from home for the first time in their lives. I am always sensitive to that student sitting unaccompanied at a cafeteria table or socially isolated in one of my classes—hoping that somehow they might make a friend so they don't feel so alone. I have been in their shoes myself three different times in my life on various university campuses. Your heart is aching, and your stomach is churning. We all need hope to live fully and fruitfully each day, especially those of us who confront the specter of loneliness or grief.

One of my favorite portions of the Bible is the description of Jesus's first encounter with Peter, who, as we know, became one of the most important of His disciples. Peter's brother Andrew, who had met Jesus before Peter did, brought his brother to talk with Jesus. This is a lesson in and of itself; we especially need to pray for and encourage our family members to come to know Jesus. The heart of this passage is what Jesus says to Peter right at the beginning of their relationship. "Jesus looked at him and said, 'You are Simon son of John. You will be called Cephas (which, when translated, is Peter'"—literally meaning "the Rock.").

In this simple exchange, Jesus offers Peter both a powerful and an intimate introduction. First, He is saying, "I know who you are, Peter. I know your birth family, your personality, your human strengths and weaknesses. I know that you will ultimately deny me." No one knows any of us more fully than the One Who made us. Second, Jesus is saying, "I know who I am making you to be, Peter. Someday, after your failure,

20

your confusion, and your disillusionment, Peter, you will be rocklike in your devotion to Me and in your mature leadership of the early Christian Church." We ought to take great comfort in the fact that Jesus knows us in all of our humanity and yet has a plan and the power to make us something much, much more than we are now.

The Lord has a great destiny and great purpose for all of our lives. Best of all, He has the power, grace, and love to make that destiny and purpose a reality. Pray that the Lord will give you His eyes to see what He is doing in the lives of those around you and His grace to encourage them in the process. We all need to look to Jesus today and to express His heart for others.

## PRAYER

*Heavenly Father, thank You for a new day to worship You and to fall in love with You all over again. Make us aware of Your Presence in our lives each moment of this day. We know that we will find fulfillment only when we pursue the purpose You have for our lives. Help us to engage in that pursuit with an undivided heart. In Jesus's name, amen.*

# BECOMING LIKE JESUS

*But we all, with unveiled faces, looking as in a mirror at
the glory of the Lord, are being transformed into the same image
from glory to glory, just as from the Lord, the Spirit.*

2 CORINTHIANS 3:18, NASB

Sometimes, when confronted with an uncomfortable or stretching command from the Lord or His Word, we can think or say to ourselves, "I am just not that kind of person." In other words, "what the Lord is asking of me might be alright for someone else with a different kind of personality or disposition, but God can't possibly expect a Christian like me to do this or that." Do we understand that the whole purpose of this "following Jesus" thing is to become a different person from the one we are now? The Lord loves us too much to leave us as He found us when He saved us from our sin. It is the mighty "self" that rails against change and stubbornly digs in against God's transformational agenda. We have not arrived yet; God is taking us to a new place to be new people. And that truly is, by definition, uncomfortable—but necessary.

How does this change occur? Is it by dint of my own effort or will? Can I speed up the transformation if I work harder at it or behave or do the right things? No! Why is it that we all understand that we are saved by grace through faith (what theologians call *justification*) but think that we become the person God wants us to be (what is called *sanctification*) through our own work and energy? It's almost as though we think we need the Lord to save us but that we can somehow become like Jesus by living right, going to church, reading the Bible, and being a "good person." The truth is that we become like Jesus in a much simpler, more profound, and more dependent manner. The apostle Paul gave the Corinthian Christians the formula for change when he wrote, as quoted above, "But we all, with unveiled faces, looking as in a mirror at the glory of the Lord, are being transformed into the same image from glory to glory, just as from the Lord, the Spirit" (2 Corinthians 3:18). The biblical truth is clear—we become what we look at. Keep your eyes on yourself and your sin—and it will be hard to get closer to being more like Jesus. Keep your eyes on trying to be a better person—and you will be spinning your wheels in a way that will simply wear you out. Instead, keep your eyes on Jesus, focus on Him, and you will become like Him. The Holy Spirit is the power source to bring about true change, not human energy or effort. At some point in time, we are inevitably going to come to the end of ourselves. Better to get there as quickly as possible so that true transformation can occur!

Of course, we do not stop praying or reading the Bible or making decisions to live in a holy manner. It's just that we stop believing that these activities will truly change us. The Holy Spirit within us transforms us, not one more attempt to "get it right." And when we fail, as we all will, we are to get up, dust ourselves off, and fix our eyes on the Lord as quickly as we can. Paul said that we need to contemplate the Lord with "unveiled" faces. What are the "veils" in my life that keep me from seeing the Lord for Who He is? How can I take those "veils" off so that I can get the most honest, powerful glimpse of Jesus possible? Change is the goal that none of us embraces with unbridled enthusiasm, and healthy change can often come slowly and sporadically, in "fits and starts," as we say. But we need to be aware that change is at the core of being a disciple of Jesus. You can't have one without the other.

P R A Y E R

*Heavenly Father, keep us from ever saying "No" to whatever change You want to work in us. We want to be more like Jesus tomorrow than we are today. We deceive ourselves so easily. Help us to see how You see us and who You are making us to be. We want our hearts to open to You with a constant "Yes," no matter what You ask of us. Help us, Lord! In Jesus's name, amen.*

# THE TRUE WORK OF GOD

*Jesus gave them this answer: "Very truly I tell you, the Son can do nothing by himself; he can do only what he sees his Father doing, because whatever the Father does the Son also does."*

JOHN 5:19

Ministry on a college campus is a uniquely ironic setting in which to speak of the love of Jesus Christ. We share with students that the grace of God, His unmerited favor, is extended to us unconditionally no matter what we do, but, at the same time, students are evaluated constantly on the basis of what they say, learn, and write. If Jesus declared that even His own works, considered in isolation, avail nothing, how much more is this true of us? Jesus made it clear that what matters is what God the Father is doing around and within us. We need to ask Him to make clear to us through the Holy Spirit on a daily basis what that is—and then get on the same page with the Father. If we think our puny accomplishments or agenda are producing anything of lasting value on their own, we are sadly mistaken. But if we are partnering with the Lord, we can bank on the fact that our efforts are contributing to fruitfulness that will last. It is futile to worry about whether we are of use to God; Jesus did not even evaluate His own life that way. Rather, we should ask: Is my life bringing glory to the Father as did the life of His Son?

Have you ever heard people say that "God helps those who help themselves," as though those words come from the Bible? Guess what. They don't! In fact, the message is contrary to what the Scripture teaches. God's grace is given to us quite apart from anything that we do—and the truth is that we can't ultimately rescue ourselves from most of the jams and difficulties we create or stumble into in our lives. Paul said it best in his letter to the churches in Ephesus: "For it is by grace you have been saved, through faith—and this not from yourselves, it is the gift of God—not by works, so that no one can boast" (2:8–9). If what I did really mattered when it came to my relationship with Jesus, then I would have the right to brag in comparison to others who are struggling in that relationship. Christians even need to be careful about talking about a *decision* to follow Jesus, as though this were a "work" that they produced through a faith they themselves have mustered. Paul's words are clear: salvation is a gift from God, as is faith. We do nothing to earn or manufacture either. The Christian band *Mercy Me*, in one of their hit songs, describes this truth not just as "good news" but rather as "the best news ever."

Does this mean that praying, reading the Bible, or obeying the Lord's commandments are unimportant or irrelevant to our walk with Jesus? Of course not. But it is a matter of getting their place and priority right in God's pattern for our lives. We cannot earn God's love by doing any of this. We can do nothing to get Him to love us more than He already does. Truth be told, some of us pray, study Scripture, or live a holy life in order to earn God's favor. We might never admit it, but we act as though He is angry with us or loves us less if we fail to do these things. I think it is fallen human instinct to believe we have to do something to clean up the mess we have made. That may be a noble impulse, but it is absolutely misdirected. Some of us think we have to earn our Heavenly Father's love in the same way we believe we have had to earn our earthly parents' love. When Jesus uttered the words "It is finished" (or "The debt has been paid") on the Cross, he was saying, at least in part, that no cleanup on our part is required.

## P R A Y E R

*Heavenly Father, thank You for what You have done by sacrificing Your Son, our Savior, on the Cross. We agree that there is nothing to be added to that holy act. Show us what You are doing around us and help us to join right in with You. Help us to nurture the relationship You have established with us. Move us to fight any interference with or obstacle to our communion and fellowship with You. Thank You for Your relentless love that seeks us out and draws us to You for Your glory and our welfare. In Jesus's name, amen.*

# HIS KINGDOM
### AND OUR MISSION

# WHAT IS THE KINGDOM
# OF GOD?

*"The time has come," [Jesus] said.*
*"The kingdom of God has come near."*
MARK 1:15

It is significant that the very first words out of the mouth of Jesus when He began His public ministry, as recorded in what is thought by many to be the oldest account, announced the advent of the Kingdom of God. He literally claimed that the Kingdom of God was near (in the words of some translations, "at hand"). Jesus never spoke haphazardly, so we know that He chose the words of His first sermon with care and endowed them with significance.

What is the Kingdom of God? People often confuse this term with an actual place or location. Indeed, the phrase "kingdom of heaven" is sometimes used interchangeably (e.g., Matthew 13:44), so it would be possible to confuse the place where we are going someday after death, if we have a saving relationship with Christ, with the idea of the Kingdom of God. But if Jesus is to be believed, the Kingdom of God is imminent—it is near. Instead, it is helpful to think of the concept of the Kingdom of God not as a place but as a realm or domain of His rulership. That is, wherever God has established His sovereignty and control, His kingdom is present. It is possible to submit my life, my relationships, my health, my finances, my decisions, and so on, to God's rule. And when I do, the Kingdom of God has come specifically there. The problem is that we live in a fallen world that is still under the influence, through my sin, your sin, and everyone else's sin, of the devil, the enemy of our souls. That is why Jesus declared that the Kingdom of God was near but had not yet fully arrived. On the Cross, Jesus accomplished what was necessary to finally defeat Satan, but that ultimate defeat has not yet been consummated. Right now on earth, the battle is raging and we live in occupied territory. We live in an "in between" time, a time in which we learn how to invite the Kingdom of God into our lives and circumstances.

And how is this invitation initiated? Through prayer. In the Gospel of Luke, chapter 11, we read that one of Jesus's disciples, witnessing the prayer of his Master, asked to be taught to pray. Of all of the different requests that could have been made based on all that they had seen Jesus do, this one demonstrates that the disciples understood the power and the priority of prayer from watching Jesus pray. Can others say that about us? Jesus's response to the request is the most famous prayer in Church history, the Lord's Prayer. In Matthew 6:10, a portion of that prayer reads, "Your kingdom come, your will be done, on earth as it is in heaven." In other words, the Lord is asking all of us to play an integral part in asking for the rule of God, His kingdom, to invade specific situations, specific relationships, and specific lives here on earth. Is someone sick? They wouldn't be sick in heaven, so I pray that the Lord might bring His kingdom to bear on the health of that person so that his or her earthly circumstances might match what they would be in heaven. Is there brokenness or pain in heaven? Then we need to pray that God's kingdom comes into the specific places where pain and brokenness dominate so that His will be done on earth as it is in heaven. I can live every day on the lookout for situations in which God's rule needs to invade and control—and then pray pinpoint prayers for His intervention. Such an understanding can bring energy and focus to our prayer lives.

## PRAYER

*Heavenly Father, alert us to the lives and situations around us that need an invasion of your power and presence. Your kingdom come in might, and Your will be dominant in us and those around us! In Jesus's name, amen.*

# A KINGDOM THAT CANNOT
# BE SHAKEN

*Therefore, since we are receiving a kingdom that cannot be shaken,
let us be thankful, and so worship God acceptably with
reverence and awe.*

HEBREWS 12:28

In Philippians 3:20–21, the apostle Paul tells his Christian friends that they are not citizens of this world but citizens of heaven. As Saint Augustine wrote in his fifth-century classic defense of Christianity, *The City of God*, there are two kingdoms that compete for our allegiance: the kingdom of this world and the Kingdom of God. You can't belong to both. Paul is making it very clear that we don't belong here; we live in a battle zone, in enemy territory. Christians compromise their witness to Christ before others to the degree that they are absorbed by their worldly loyalties, concerns, and pursuits. We cannot and should not live in such a way that we avoid interactions with the people around us who are hurting and broken in a world under the thumb of Satan. Jesus Himself prayed that we would not be taken out of the world, but He also acknowledged that, like Him, we are not of the world (John 17:15–16). Finding the balance Jesus prayed is a lifelong challenge for one who wants to be His disciple. How distinctive is my life? How distinctive is yours? Paul compared the life of a Christian to stars in a dark night sky (Philippians 2:15). Is it that clear to those around us that our life belongs to Jesus and nothing in this world?

In a world that shakes all around us and in which stability and consistency elude us, the writer of Hebrews declared that the Kingdom of God we are receiving cannot be shaken. Given that truth, he encouraged his readers to be thankful and worship God with the reverence and awe He rightfully deserves (12:28). The next verse tells us that God is a consuming fire; if we are building our life with less than God's best, it could go up in smoke. But any decision or investment grounded in the power and reality of God's rule, His kingdom, cannot be shaken. Let's agree to ask the Lord to weigh our lives and to root out anything that is less than His best for us. Let's act from the truth that we don't belong in this world but have been sent here as missionaries to bring the light and love and hope of our King to those oppressed and suffering under the domination of the enemy. That is the great purpose appointed to the subjects of the Kingdom of God.

P R A Y E R

---

*Heavenly Father, thank You that You are in control—even if it may not seem that way to us. Help us to invite Your rule into our lives and the lives of those around us in specific ways this coming week. So dominate our lives, Lord, that those around us recognize that we are different, that our home is not in this world but with You. In Jesus's name, amen.*

# MOSES IS DEAD

*"Moses my servant is dead. Now then, you and all these people,*
*get ready to cross the Jordan River into the land I am*
*about to give to them."*
JOSHUA 1:2

It can be both fascinating and confusing to reflect on why God sometimes brings the obvious to our attention. Certainly, Joshua was well aware that Moses was dead; God didn't need to tell him. In fact, Joshua was probably very apprehensive over the fact that now his mentor Moses was gone, and he was in charge. But maybe that is why God stated the obvious—to acknowledge "the elephant in the room," as the old saying goes—that is, to get Joshua's hesitation or fear out on the table where God could deal with it. The Lord was telling Joshua that he was about to enter a new era of ministry. Things would not be the same.

Not only was Moses dead, but the way God had used Moses or worked through Moses was also gone. Joshua was not to expect that God would continue to operate just as He had in the past; God's ways are not to be taken for granted as an established pattern. For example, God separated the Red Sea *in front of Moses,* while he would later stop the flow of the Jordan River upstream *before Joshua and the people.* We would do well to come to God every day with the expectation that He will surprise us with the way He loves us and demonstrates His grace toward us. He is God; we are not. He is in control; we are not.

Moses may have been dead—but that didn't interrupt or derail God's intention for the people of Israel. The mission remained the same—and God was ready for Joshua to move on. He said to Joshua, "Now then, . . ." God is sensitive to our losses and the changes in life that can send us into a tailspin. But at some point we hear His "Now then, . . ." and know that it is time to press toward completion of the purpose for which we have been called. And that purpose is to move into the place of promise that the Lord has for each of us—whether Israel so long ago or us right now. Joshua was told that God would never leave or forsake him, as he had never left Moses, in the process of leading His people into their land of promise (Joshua 1:5). God will never leave us as we move on, either. He will see us through to the end. Paul told Timothy that "I know whom [God] I have believed, and am convinced that he is able to guard what I have entrusted to him [my life and its purpose] until that day" (2 Timothy 1:12)—the day when Jesus returns to take us to the place He is preparing for us.

What does God require of us when we hear the "Now then, . . ." and move on? To be strong and courageous. God tells Joshua to be strong and courageous three times in the following five verses of Joshua, chapter one. Perhaps Joshua didn't feel very strong and courageous in the wake of Moses's death; he was thrust into a leadership role for which he might have felt ill-prepared. But the grounds for our strength and courage must never be our estimation of our own experience or resources. Our strength and courage arise out of the reality of the Lord's presence in our lives—not anything that we bring to the situation ourselves. Paul told the Corinthian church that God loves to use broken "jars of clay" like us to carry out His purposes so that everyone will see that "this all-surpassing power is from God and not from us" (2 Corinthians 4:7). Our prospects are infinitely more positive than we often believe because they depend upon God working through us, not on our own work.

P R A Y E R

*Heavenly Father, something may feel dead in our lives, just as Joshua may have felt as he faced life without Moses. You understand our pain, our uncertainty, our fears. Thank You for loving us so gently when we hurt so dramatically. When You are ready for us to move on, help us to be ready to move on. And give us the strength and courage we need to serve Your purpose for our lives. Thank You that You are with us always as You lead us to our place of promise. In Jesus's name, amen.*

# OUR CALL TO MISSION

*"Wait for the gift my Father promised."*
ACTS 1:4

Imagine the emotional roller-coaster ride of those first disciples. They had invested their lives, leaving behind everything, for three years in Jesus's ministry. Jesus entered Jerusalem triumphantly, as a King, so their hopes were high. But by the end of the week, Jesus had been arrested and then executed in the most disreputable manner possible at the time. Not only were the hopes of the disciples crushed, but they were disillusioned, on the run, and theologically confused—Deuteronomy 21:23 taught that anyone who was hung on a cross was cursed by God. They were scattered by persecution until they started to hear rumors of Jesus's "appearances"— more confusion! When Jesus did appear to them, their minds were confounded by the range of possibilities—was He a ghost, a man, or something in between? Then Jesus ascended into heaven before their very eyes (so they would clearly understand He was gone), leaving His followers with one dominant question: *Now what do we do?*

First, Jesus told His followers to *wait*. Oh no, please not that! Anything but that word! Everything about us as human beings tends toward the desire to propel ourselves into action. In fact, we probably ought to be called human "doings" rather than human "beings." We tend to "do" much better than we "be"—er, let's make that "are." The concept of waiting was even harder when Jesus added the words "for the gift my Father promised" (Acts 1:4). The phrase conjures up memories for me of desperate Christmas Eves when, as children, my sisters and I could hardly sleep waiting on the gifts Santa might bring us on Christmas morning. And, of course, there was always the parallel effort to discover the identity of the actual gift we were waiting to open. In this case, the disciples knew they were waiting on the Holy Spirit. And they were waiting actively, not complacently, meeting together and praying in the days leading up to Pentecost. Their focus was never on the gift, but on the Giver—knowing that any gift that comes from the Father is good.

Second, in Acts 1:8, Jesus told His disciples that they would be *witnesses* in the new time and new place He was bringing them into. Notice that this was not His command but a simple statement of fact. A witness is someone who speaks from personal knowledge about facts and their significance to the issues at hand. The Lord's intent is not to teach us something so much as it is to make us the incarnation of what we are preaching or speaking. Where does the power originate to be a witness? Not from emotions—they won't last. Not from our intelligence or ingenuity—they are not sufficient. Being a witness is too hard and too expansive to be achieved through our own flesh, will, or efforts. It requires the power of the Holy Spirit. All we are called to do is to show others that we belong to Jesus and that He has made all of the difference in our lives.

Finally, at the end of Acts, chapter one, the disciples worked to *keep the group together and to find new leaders.* Dynamic episodes, times of change, can sow the seeds of discord and division. Indeed, in the days between the crucifixion and the resurrection appearances of Jesus, the disciples had scattered. Now, however, Acts 1:14 declares that the disciples were praying together in one accord. We need to fight for unity in our families, in our churches, and in our communities. And we need to always be on the lookout to encourage new, especially younger, leaders. Peter told the other disciples that betrayal and death can never disrupt the plans of God. In this case, they actually fulfilled His strategy.

## PRAYER

*Heavenly Father, all we want to do is reflect Your life to the greatest degree possible—help us to get out of the way so that others can catch an unobstructed glimpse of Jesus in us. Give us grace to wait when You call us to rest and trust in You. Fill us full of the Holy Spirit so that our lives may be empowered by Your Presence. In Jesus's name, amen.*

# THEREFORE, GO . . .

*"Surely I am with you always, to the very end of the age."*
MATTHEW 28:20

L ike most of us, I used to believe that missionaries were those special people God called to "far off places" where no one really wanted to go. But because these missionaries were such exceptional people, they were willing to make the sacrifice, often living in primitive conditions in jungles or deserts. In fact, truth be told, when I was younger I prayed more than once that the Lord wouldn't send me to Africa—or some other place I didn't really want to go!

Fortunately, both my spiritual maturity and my understanding of the nature of God's call on our lives has grown to the point that I now realize that we are all missionaries if we choose to be. Some of us serve groups of people who are not like us, so our experience is more cross-cultural, but God has sent all of us "out" to share our love for Him and our faith in Him with other people. Remember the very last words of Jesus recorded by the Gospel writer Matthew: "Therefore, go and make disciples of all nations, baptizing them in the name of the Father and of the Son and of the Holy Spirit, and teaching them to obey everything I have commanded you. And surely I am with you always, to the very end of the age" (Matthew 28:19–20). I still believe that missionaries are special people who make sacrifices that not everyone is willing to make to serve the Lord. And that is how I feel about every Christian who prioritizes their passion to do whatever God has called them to do on a daily basis, even when no one is watching other than the Lord, and no one is applauding or cheering them on. Let me share a couple of important missionary principles.

First, *the motivation for our missionary service is the command of the Lord and not the needs of the people we serve.* Simply put, we go because, as Jesus declared in the Great Commission, we are called to go and make disciples of all nations. Unfortunately, many people go because of the obvious needs of the people they will serve rather than as the basic act of obedience required by the Lord's command. The problem in being motivated by the needs of others is that the world is full of needy people. We will exhaust ourselves trying to meet all of the needs that we know about in this world. And we won't have a clear understanding of how to prioritize one set of needs over another if we are driven primarily by the desire to help people. I'm not saying we shouldn't want to help people, but we are missionaries because we are sent by God, not drawn by need. If we focus on the assignment God has given us, we will have a specific sense of where we are to serve and to whom we are to go—rather than running around in a chaotic fashion, scrambling to meet every need we perceive. If you aren't sure where the Lord has called you to serve, ask Him in prayer.

Second, God's only *real call to a missionary is to trust what Jesus has said and done.* We are not called to do or to be anything else. We need to stand in the sufficient position of limitless confidence in Christ Jesus. Jesus told us that He would always be with us! Isn't that enough? He also declared, "All authority in heaven and on earth has been given to me." If the Lord will never leave us alone and has all authority to deal with all circumstances we encounter each day, we have all that we need to serve the Lord fruitfully as His missionaries.

## PRAYER

*Heavenly Father, we eagerly respond to Your call to go and make disciples of all nations. We are motivated by Your call, not by the needs that swirl around us. Direct our steps so that we purposefully serve specifically where You want us to serve. Help us to trust You with all of our hearts and count on Your power and Presence to meet each circumstance we encounter this week. Our lives are all about You, Lord, not about us or anyone else. In Jesus's name, amen.*

# THE POWER OF
## A BROKEN LIFE

# TELLING OUR STORY

*They triumphed over him [Satan] by the blood of the Lamb and by the word of their testimony.*

REVELATION 12:11

We have two weapons to use to overcome the lies and the accusations of Satan, the enemy of our souls: Jesus's shed blood on the Cross and our own story of what God has done in our lives through the application of Jesus's atoning sacrifice for us. Jesus died for all of us on the Cross, but we need to appropriate that act of grace uniquely and allow His redemption to change us and give us a song to sing and a story to tell. We may not be Bible scholars or be able to defend the great doctrines of the Christian faith through theological explanations. But each one of us has a story of what the Lord has done in our lives that no one can dispute. And we owe it to the Lord and to others to tell that story whenever we can.

Oftentimes, our stories involve brokenness, heartache, failure, weakness, or shame. We have to allow the Lord to show us when it is appropriate and important to be vulnerable to sharing that part of our story. Ernest Hemingway once wrote, "The world breaks everyone, and afterward, many are stronger at the broken places." It is the broken people who can be trusted, the ones who have learned that self-sufficiency is a myth and that the Lord will comfort and heal us at those points where we have fallen or been shattered. When we are broken or suffering, we have a choice as to how we will respond. We can either blame God and others, or we can reach up to the Lord for help even when we don't have an inkling of what is going on or what He might be up to. With the choice made, we will become either *bitter* or *better*. The only difference in the result is the letter *I*—if I can die to self, God can use me to share His grace with others who might be broken or struggling in the same way I am.

Paul told the Corinthian church in his second letter to them: "Praise be to the God and Father of our Lord Jesus Christ, the Father of compassion and the God of all comfort, who comforts us in all our troubles, so that we can comfort those in any trouble with the comfort we ourselves receive from God" (1:3–4). Don't be surprised if God has you sharing your particular story of brokenness time and time again with others going through similar circumstances. And when we do, we need to follow the instructions of 1 Peter 3:15—share our story with gentleness and respect—not with coercion or manipulation, leaving people free to respond as they wish. As Paul told Timothy (2 Timothy 4:2), we need to share "in season and out of season," when we feel like it and when we don't, when it is convenient and when it isn't.

The Jewish Levites and priests asked John the Baptist who he was. He said, "I am a voice." He basically was saying that he had a story to share. He explained to them that He was speaking in the midst of a *desert*—a world dry, overheated, and worn out with its own confusions, frustrations, hostility, and hopelessness. And the story of this man in the desert was simple: "Clear out all of the obstacles, walls, and barricades, the ups and the downs, that are keeping you from receiving what the Lord has for you." John put it this way: "Make straight the way of the Lord." We need to tell people the same thing, using our stories as the best example we know of the truth of the love and the power of our heavenly Father. You don't have to appear on a television show to gain status as "The Voice." Jesus will give us lots of opportunities this week if we will just stay alert to what He is doing around us.

## PRAYER

*Heavenly Father, thank You for the way that You have saved us, healed us, comforted us, strengthened us, and been to us what we have needed You to be. Help us to tell others about You and what You have been to us and done for us. Sometimes we are fearful and need courage or confidence. Please give us a Holy Spirit "shot in the arm" at those moments. You have great purpose for all of us and have provided for us so richly over and over again. Give us the words to tell others about the hope You have given us through the love You have shown us. In Jesus's name, amen.*

# WRESTLING WITH GOD

*So Jacob was left alone, and a man wrestled
with him till daybreak.*

GENESIS 32:24

God cares about names; they are endowed with great meaning. In the Old Testament, the names of God describe His character. As *Yahweh* or "I Am," for example, He is the God who is eternally present. As *Jehovah Jireh*, He is the Lord Who provides for His children. The names of His followers are no less important. And when a name is changed in Scripture, we ought to sit up and take notice because a shift in identity is occurring. Such was the case with the patriarch Jacob, grandson of Abraham. The younger brother, by only minutes, of Esau, Jacob had actively deceived his father, Isaac, in order to steal his older brother's blessing. Fearing for his life, Jacob, whose name literally meant "he grasps the heel" (exactly what he had been doing to his twin brother at birth), a Hebrew idiom for "he deceives," ran away from home to live with his uncle.

Returning home years later meant that Jacob would have to face his brother, Esau, once again. Fearing for his life and the life of his family, Jacob sent ahead a series of gifts in the way of livestock, hoping that Esau might be pacified by the gifts before he actually saw Jacob himself (Genesis 32:20). Jacob also sent his family on ahead of himself to protect them, so that he was left all alone the night before he met Esau. The Scripture tells us that Jacob wrestled with a man (later identified as an angel; Jacob called the being God himself) throughout the night and that the man could not overpower Jacob. At daybreak, the angel told Jacob to let him go, but Jacob refused until he had received from Him a blessing. At this point, the Lord changed Jacob's name to "Israel," which meant one who struggles or wrestles with God. The blessing Jacob received from God was the name change, the character change, indicating that the life of Jacob, now Israel, would be forever different because he had been struggling with God all alone. The wrestling match did cost Jacob something. He came away from the encounter with a displaced hip and limped due to this injury (Genesis 32:22–32).

In the Bible, any follower of the Lord, whether or not they are Jewish, is considered a descendant of Abraham, Isaac, and Jacob—and therefore is called an Israelite. In other words, God's people are identified forever as those who wrestle or struggle with God. A real, authentic relationship with the Lord inevitably leads us through those times in our lives when we struggle with God due to fear, doubt, and even selfishness on our parts. Sometimes we struggle with Him simply because we do not understand His ways. The prophet Isaiah proclaimed, "'For my thoughts are not your thoughts, neither are your ways my ways,' declares the LORD" (Isaiah 55:8). The story of Jacob shows us that it is okay to wrestle with God—and that He will show us mercy in the process. Please notice that the angel allowed Jacob to survive and even prevail to a degree. I suspect that the Lord did what we often do with our children in various games: He let Jacob win. Because of the struggle, the faith of Jacob, now Israel, was his own—real and authentic.

Life can leave us with a limp. Our frailty and weakness remind us that we need the Lord. And the limp produces a compassionate heart for the struggle of others. It is just such people God uses to accomplish His mission of love and redemption. And Jacob's story has a happy ending. It seems that Jacob was not the only one who changed in this saga. Esau forgave his brother and did not take vengeance on him for his prior deceitfulness. Israel, the one who wrestled with God, got a second chance to do what was right in relation to his family. Our God is a God of second chances. So, if you feel as though you are all alone in the middle of an emotional or spiritual night, don't be afraid to wrestle with God. Tell Him about your doubts, your fears, your anger, and your anguish. He will not overpower you. You will no doubt walk away from the struggle very aware of your weakness and humanity. But You will be changed by the encounter, and God will ultimately give you the gift of faith that will allow you to serve Him no matter what you have done in the past.

## PRAYER

*Heavenly Father, sometimes we don't understand what You are up to in our lives and You feel very far away from us. Cause us to be honest with You rather than pretending we don't feel frustration and pain. Stay with us all through the nights of our loneliness and change us in the process. Thank You that You are willing to use us and work through us in spite of all of our weakness and selfishness. We love You with all that we are! In Jesus's name, amen.*

# DEFEATING FEAR

*Have mercy on me, my God, have mercy on me, for in you*
*I take refuge. I will take refuge in the shadow of your wings*
*until the disaster has passed. I cry out to God Most High, to*
*God, who vindicates me. He sends from heaven and saves me,*
*rebuking those who hotly pursue me—God sends forth his*
*love and his faithfulness . . . My heart, O God, is steadfast,*
*my heart is steadfast; I will sing and make music . . .*
*For great is your love, reaching to the heavens; your*
*faithfulness reaches to the skies. Be exalted, O God,*
*above the heavens; let your glory be over all the earth.*

PSALM 57:1–3, 7, 10–11

Fear is a daunting opponent for many who seek to follow Jesus. All of us have had times in our lives when we were limited, even imprisoned, by a real sense of apprehension. If you study the Scriptures, you will find that the Lord did not attempt to present a picture there of people who were always brave and courageous in the face of frightening challenges. The Bible tells us the stories of real-life people who battled fear and, at times, were dominated by it. We have such a picture in Psalm 57. The introduction to the psalm tells us that it was written while David was hiding in a cave from King Saul who was trying to kill him. It is safe to say that David was frightened, among other emotions, in this predicament.

In the face of a pursuit by the king of Israel that could have ended with his death, hiding in a cave, David offers us insight into how to handle fear. Think about these principles:

- *Seek safety and refuge, both physically and spiritually.* David, in his vulnerability, was wise to seek a place of protection. All of us have our safe places, emotionally and physically, and we shouldn't be ashamed to retreat to them during times of trial and distress. Identifying the Lord as our ultimate place of refuge is wisdom when we are beset with fear—until the disaster we fear has passed. And then the Lord must remain our refuge.

- *The Lord has a purpose for us that He will fulfill in spite of our fear.* Your fright does not disqualify you from being used by God in the special and unique way He has designed for you in advancing His will and way in and through you.
- *God is faithful in His love for me—a love that is a real, rich resource.* The truth is that His love for me is bigger and more real than the fear I am tasting. Fear always appears bigger than it actually is—sort of like a shadow dwarfing the object it is cast by.
- *My heart must remain steadfast.* David acknowledges and repeats that his heart is steadfast even as he experiences fear in that cave. It is as though he is saying, "I may be frightened, but my heart is locked onto God's goodness, love, power, and ultimate rescue."
- *It wouldn't hurt to sing out loud.* Do a study sometime on the power of song, especially during times of trouble, as demonstrated in the Bible. You will find, time and time again, that people who sing in the face of fear and danger find their release and rescue waiting right around the corner. The enemy knows this power is released in song, and so he gets us thinking that our voices are of poor quality or that others don't want to hear us singing. I am not writing about simply "whistling in the dark," wishing that something would change. I am speaking of employing a proven spiritual principle in our lives.

If you are plagued by fear, let David's psalm (57) be your guide. Your heavenly Father does not want you to be limited by that fear. He wants you to be absolutely free to serve Him in freedom and wholeness.

## PRAYER

*Lord, thank You that the Bible is a book depicting real people who teach us what it means to follow You in real life. Increase our faith this week, and give us grace to defeat fear in our experience. We take our refuge in You, Father, and we rely upon Your unlimited, all-powerful love for us every minute of every day. In Jesus's name, amen.*

# THE TOUCH OF JESUS

*"Lord, if you are willing, you can make me clean."*
MATTHEW 8:2

We have all had the sensation of real loneliness and isolation at certain points in our lives. I moved to university campuses in Virginia, California, and Tennessee at various stages of my life and knew no one there each time when I first arrived. California was particularly hard, since it was so far away from my home in Indiana and the friends I had made during my undergraduate years at the College of William and Mary in Williamsburg, Virginia. I flew to Pasadena, California, for the very first time in the fall of 1979 to attend Fuller Theological Seminary; I had never been to Pasadena before the day that I traveled there to begin school and wasn't even sure which bus from the airport would take me to campus. That first night in California, without a car, I remember walking to a fairly dirty little drive-in restaurant (I learned later that there were plenty of good places to eat nearby) and had a difficult time swallowing the greasy hamburger I had ordered. I was really choked up and quite emotional over being so very far away from family and friends. All I wanted was a little human companionship.

What is Jesus's heart for the lonely and isolated? I think we can see it in a very poignant story found in the eighth chapter of the Gospel of Matthew, verses 1–4. After finishing his Sermon on the Mount, Jesus came down from the mountain and immediately crossed paths with a male leper. Leprosy is a hideous disease that causes people to lose appendages, like toes, fingers, and even noses and ears. It is a highly contagious disease as well, so no one would ever come near to a leper, let alone touch one. During New Testament times, as well as later, in the Middle Ages, lepers were forced to travel in packs, wearing bells around their necks or shouting "Unclean" so that people would know they were coming and could hide from them as they passed by.

Leprosy was not only a physical disease—it was a condition of humiliation and isolation. The leper in this instance tells Jesus that he believes that Jesus can heal him "if he is willing." Anyone who has read the Gospel narratives and is familiar with the character of Jesus will be startled by the leper's genuine concern that Jesus might not be willing to heal him. Depending on the extent of his knowledge of Jesus and His ways, I suspect that the leper's doubt about Jesus's willingness had more to do with how he had been shunned by other people than by any genuine question mark about Jesus's nature of mercy and compassion. The leper may have reasoned, "People in general won't get near me. Why should this holy man be any different?"

Jesus not only defies the leper's expectations by expressing His willingness to heal the man; He makes a move that would have stunned witnesses present at the scene. Jesus reached out and touched the man (verse 3). Can you imagine what it would have felt like for this man who hadn't experienced physical contact with another human possibly for years to be touched by Jesus? A man suffering such severe tactile deprivation would have experienced sensory "fireworks" when Jesus offered this simple but powerful expression of love.

We are unlikely to encounter any individuals suffering from the physical condition of leprosy during the course of our daily routine. But I suspect we might cross paths with someone so stigmatized by a behavior, a failure, a reputation, a background, or an inability to function in a healthy manner socially that they have become a virtual, emotional, and social leper or pariah. Jesus needs to touch these people through us. We need to show the isolated and the lonely Jesus's heart of compassion for them. We need to pray that the Lord will show us who these people are and will give us the grace and the sensitivity to reach out to them with the Master's touch.

## PRAYER

*Heavenly Father, we pray just that—show us these people and give us Your heart for them. Lead us to people hungering for human companionship and allow us to love them toward You. Touch them through us and draw them into the community of Your disciples. In Jesus's name, amen.*

# INVESTING IN THE
# PROMISES OF GOD

*"I bought the field at Anathoth from my cousin Hanamel."*
JEREMIAH 32:9

It is not surprising that many of the images or word pictures found in the Bible are from the Old Testament, especially the writings of the ancient prophets. In the opening verse of Jeremiah 32, we find that the prophet Jeremiah had been imprisoned in the royal palace of Judah by his own king, Zedekiah. It seems that Jeremiah had been prophesying that the Babylonians would soon capture the city and even take Zedekiah with them back to Babylon. The fall of Jerusalem, according to the prophecy of Jeremiah, was rooted in the continual disobedience and faithlessness of the people of Judah—and God was punishing them for their sin. Zedekiah no doubt saw Jeremiah's preaching as demoralizing, since the Babylonians were literally right outside Jerusalem building siege ramps against the city walls.

In the midst of this chaos and Jeremiah's imprisonment, the Lord told the prophet to do a very strange thing. He told him to buy a piece of property nearby from his cousin. Given his own prophecy of the impending doom of the city and a 70-year exile for the Jewish people in Babylon, investing in a field did not make a lot of sense. Still, Jeremiah did what the Lord told him to do. Then Jeremiah placed the property deed in a clay jar so that it would last a long time. Following this action that provides the word picture, Jeremiah spoke these words: "For this is what the LORD Almighty, the God of Israel, says: Houses, fields and vineyards will again be bought in this land" (verse 15). While the circumstances surrounding Jeremiah were grim, God had given him hope that things would get better and that, one day, the people would return to this land. God was calling Jeremiah to invest in His promise even at the darkest moment of doubt and uncertainty.

We all face really challenging times and situations when it seems as though all hope is lost and the enemy surrounds us. At that point, can we hear the Lord reminding us that He is with us and that there is a future of promise, peace, and breakthrough somewhere up ahead? If we believe that, how can we "stake a claim" on that future? How, like Jeremiah, can we invest in God's promise in a way that might seem contrary to the flow of events around us? I am not sure what the answer to those questions might be, but I suspect that the Lord would speak to us about them if we were to ask Him.

After Jeremiah bought the field, He prayed to the Lord in a simple and honest manner: "Ah, Sovereign LORD, you have made the heavens and the earth by your great power and outstretched arm. Nothing is too hard for you" (verse 17). Because nothing is too hard for the Lord, we can have faith that He can turn the really awful times of our lives around. We may have to wait; the children of Israel waited 70 years to come back to rebuild Jerusalem. And we may not understand why we are having such a hard time in the first place. But we can be certain of the Lord's character and love for us. He will rebuild our lives. He will restore our fortunes. He will lead us into the future with hope. We can trust Him. He loves us as though each one of us is the only one in the world to be loved.

## P R A Y E R

*Heavenly Father, give us faith and hope when all seems to be crumbling around us. Show us how we can act in faith at the moment when all seems lost. Cause us to see You in the midst of our sorrows and trials. Carry us when we can't move forward under our own power. Thank You for the bright future You have for us up ahead and for Your love for us that we often don't perceive, acknowledge, understand, or appreciate. Give us grace to embrace the fact that the same power that made resurrection Sunday possible after a dark, deadly Friday is available to each of us in our own valleys of the shadow of death. In the name of the risen Savior, Jesus Christ, we ask this. Amen.*

# COMMUNITY
# CONNECTIONS

# GO BEFORE IT'S TOO LATE

*Do your best to come to me quickly.*
2 TIMOTHY 4:9

It is very possible that we will fail to understand or grasp when those moments arrive that represent an opportunity that will be lost forever if not pursued. For example, we don't really know when that last time will come for us to talk to a loved one and tell them we love them before they are gone. Even high school or college friends can be lost to us in terms of a vibrant relationship when one or the other of us moves away and we lose touch due to the demands and routines of ordinary life—almost without noticing when it is happening. Timothy, the young pastor who served as the right-hand man of the apostle Paul, faced such a moment when he received a letter from his elderly mentor who was imprisoned in Rome.

Just as we can fail to recognize or anticipate the significance of a certain day in our lives, it might have been easy to overlook the urgency of the request Paul was making of Timothy, tucked away as it was in a laundry list of instructions at the end of his second letter to his young colleague. It may have helped that Paul wrote the same words twice—whenever anything appears in the Bible twice in a short span of verses, we need to pay attention to what the Holy Spirit is telling us. Paul asked Timothy to be sure to "come to me quickly" and again to "do your best to get here before winter."

Why is this important? Scholars disagree about when this epistle was written, but most certainly it was near the end of Paul's earthly life. It could have been written around A.D. 61, during what would have been Paul's only imprisonment in Rome. Or it could have been written in 65 during a second imprisonment in the imperial capital following a missionary journey to Spain unmentioned in the New Testament book of Acts but believed by many Church history experts to have occurred. Either way, Paul's death was imminent. Depending on when Timothy received and read this letter, the window of time available to him to find a ship to travel to Rome during the season when sea travel was possible (weather-wise) might have been very brief. Had he hesitated at all, he might not have arrived before Paul was beheaded (according to Church tradition) during the persecution launched against the early Church by the Roman Emperor Nero. Timothy may have had no idea that he needed to heed Paul's encouragement to come quickly, before winter, or it might already have been too late to ever again talk with his mentor face-to-face. In fact, we don't know for sure whether Timothy actually arrived in time to have one last meeting with his friend on this side of heaven.

Just a few sentences before his final instructions to Timothy, Paul wrote these words: "I have fought the good fight, I have finished the race, I have kept the faith" (verse 7). Paul affirmed that, because he had remained true, the Lord had a crown of righteousness in store for him and anyone "who has longed for his [Jesus's] appearing" (verse 8). Paul was a triumphant apostle who was ready to go home to be with the Lord, and I believe he knew that the time would come soon for that home-going. People near the time of their deaths will sometimes have a sense of the proximity of that moment. No doubt the apostle Paul had this kind of spiritual premonition. I hope Timothy recognized his need to go quickly to be at the side of his spiritual father. I pray that we will all recognize those Holy Spirit inspired nudges that we need to tell someone this week that we love them. Or maybe there is a relationship in my life that has been strained or severed, and I need to act *now* to do my part to redirect it toward reconciliation. Let's not wait too long; let's come quickly, before winter, . . . before it's too late. If we will just pay attention to the Lord and to what others are saying to us, we can discern the moments and the opportunities that we will never have again.

## PRAYER

*Heavenly Father, is there anyone this week to whom I need to reach out with Your love and compassion? Is there a relationship in my life that is ripe for a renewed effort to bring healing and hope? Please help me not to miss the opportunity You are affording me. Help us to fight the good fight, to finish the race You have set before us, and to keep the faith. We long for Your appearing and to hear these special words from You: "Well done, good and faithful servant." In Jesus's name, amen.*

# PEOPLE ARE THE PRIORITY

*The Lord stood at my side and gave me strength.*

2 TIMOTHY 4:17

In the final verses of Paul's second letter to Timothy, the elderly apostle is describing his relationships with some people whom he has loved deeply; some who have hurt him deeply; some who have disappointed him; and others who have remained faithful to him through all of the years, and trials, of his earthly life. The fact that Paul's last words to Timothy focused on people shows us what following Jesus is all about. It is about serving the Lord through serving others. It is about showing everyone, as only the Lord makes possible, the love of Jesus and the truth of His Word. Who were some of the people to whom Paul's mind turned during his time alone in that Roman prison?

Some people, like Demas in verse 9, desert us because "love for this world" and all of the temporary delights it has to offer overwhelm their commitment to walk in the company of Christ-followers. Like Paul, we are separated from others at times just because the circumstances demand it, as was the case for Crescens and Titus (verse 10). We may even encourage others to leave us so that they can fulfill the call of Christ on their lives in other places; Paul sent Tychicus to Ephesus for that reason (verse 12).

Many scholars believe that Alexander the metalworker may have been the individual who turned in Paul to the Roman authorities (verse 14). Paul warned Timothy to steer clear of this man and his opposition to the gospel. At the same time, Paul asked Timothy, who was in Ephesus (modern day Turkey), to bring Mark (full name John Mark) with him when he came to Rome (verse 11). This little verse is so significant! Paul and Barnabas had argued over Mark's loyalty after this young man had gone home early from their first missionary journey. Paul refused to depend upon Mark during his second trip and took Silas as a companion instead. The Scripture does not tell us why Mark had abandoned Paul and Barnabas in Pamphylia (Acts 13:13), but broken relationships for Paul with both the young man and with

Barnabas resulted from the incident. Now, older, wiser, and more patient, Paul had forgiven John Mark and wanted to see him again. Is there anyone in our lives to whom we need to give a second, or twentieth, chance? Is the Lord calling us to forgive someone "after all this time" because reconciliation is more important than whatever produced the conflict in the first place? God doesn't call us to pretend the hurt never happened, but I do believe He will give us the grace and the power to forgive if we ask Him.

Clearly, beyond his allegiance to Jesus Christ, Paul's chief concern was for people and relationships. These verses are filled with even more names I have not mentioned in this devotion: Paul's faithful friends and ministry partners Priscilla and Aquila, Onesiphorus, Erastus, Trophimus, Eubulus, Pudens, Linus, Claudia, and all the brothers (verses 19–21). I imagine the aged apostle sitting in the darkness and the quiet of his Roman prison cell, thinking about all of the people he had known; served; encouraged; warned; rebuked; and, above all, loved through so many years of ministry. And I am sure that Paul was proud of what the Lord had done in the lives of most of the people he had been privileged to serve through the Lord's calling, grace, and empowerment. We do well to make serving people our first priority. I suspect that God has placed special individuals in all of our lives who are gifts from God. We need to thank Him for them!

## PRAYER

*Heavenly Father, thank You that we are never alone. You are always with us and have surrounded us with others to encourage and strengthen us. Remind us today who these dear people are and guide us to pray for them gratefully, compassionately, and fervently. In Jesus's name, amen.*

# THE KING'S
# POTTERY SERVICE

*These were the potters and those who dwelt among plants
and hedges: there they dwelt with the king for his work.*

1 CHRONICLES 4:23, KJ21

There are times when the Holy Spirit will teach us through more obscure biblical passages that might seem, on the surface, to lack any relevance to our lives. One such verse from the Old Testament book of 1 Chronicles is printed above. This little gem is found in the midst of nine chapters of genealogies. I find it tempting sometimes to just skip over the chapters in the Bible that constitute seemingly endless lists of names. There are two problems with jumping past such passages. First, all of these names remind us that the Lord is a lover of people. He cares about all of us and knows us each by name. Second, we will miss the understated parenthetical treasures tucked into these lists if we don't read them.

All of us have the opportunity to be "potters" who work for the king. In Jeremiah 18, the prophet likens the Lord to a potter who is shaping all of our lives in a beautiful way to serve His purposes for us. Isaiah makes the same comparison in his prophecy: "Yet you, LORD, are our Father. We are the clay; you are the potter; we are all the work of your hand" (64:8). First Chronicles 4:23 reminds us all that we can be potters, too, working in the King's service. We can shape our own lives and the lives of others in a way that will glorify our King and advance His kingdom. Indeed, our sole purpose is to dwell with King Jesus for His work. We have no personal agenda apart from that goal; this is to be a way of life for us. Can we be spiritual shapers and molders who encourage and influence others to put the Lord first in their thoughts, words, and actions?

The opportunity and challenge of being this kind of person are disclosed above, in 1 Chronicles 4:23. We are surrounded by growing things—plants and hedges. That is the opportunity. I'm not talking about literal plants and hedges unless you are a farmer, landscape worker, or florist. But the people around us are capable of so much growth if we will only water them with kindness, graciousness, patience, and gentleness. People are literally starving for strength and encouragement, for the knowledge that others believe in them and the purposeful possibilities God has planted in their lives. Weeds can sometimes grow, too, in our lives; it is good to have those people who will gently help us see that those weeds need to be pulled out of our hearts—and have the sense to know that the Lord is the One who needs to do the weeding, according to His timetable. The challenge of being a potter in the King's service is that the plants and hedges we live among can sometimes obstruct or limit our vision. It may be hard to see what God is doing in our lives or in the lives of others. Hedges were used on the grounds of some European castles to form complex mazes through which people wandered. Maybe you feel as though you are lost in a maze right now and have no idea how to live your own life, let alone be a positive mentor (a potter) for another person. In those circumstances, we need to ask the heavenly Potter to shape us and others according to His will without demanding an explanation of the process or an advance glimpse of the final product.

## PRAYER

*Heavenly Father, more than anything else, we want to work with You and serve Your purposes in our lives and in the lives of others. Help us to be good mentors and sources of encouragement to those around us. We might not be able to see clearly what You are doing, but we trust that You are a good God Who loves us more than we can possibly imagine. Have Your way with us this week. In Jesus's name, amen.*

# A CHILD WILL LEAD THEM

*People were bringing little children to Jesus for him to place
his hands on them, but the disciples rebuked them. When
Jesus saw this, he was indignant. He said to them, "Let the
little children come to me, and do not hinder them, for the
kingdom of God belongs to such as these. Truly I tell you,
anyone who will not receive the kingdom of God like a
little child will never enter it." And he took the children in
his arms, placed his hands on them and blessed them.*

MARK 10:13–16

You can tell a lot about a person by the way they treat those around them who are essentially powerless and without defense. In particular, the way that a person treats children and animals is very telling. In the passage above, the people bringing the children to Jesus appreciated the value of those children and desired that the children receive all that God had for them in the way of a blessing. The disciples, on the other hand, minimized the value of those children. Maybe they saw them as an interruption in Jesus's busy schedule, or perhaps they perceived each of them, as was common in their culture, as being "not quite a person," as deserving less of the attention of the Master than full-grown or fully developed people. Too often our society concurs with the disciples. Some people in generations not too long past would remark with poor judgment, "Children should be seen and not heard"—as though they are dashboard ornaments on the interstate highway of life. But more significantly and tragically, the number of abortions in this country and the abuse that children routinely suffer emotionally and even sexually at the hands of very sick and broken adults demonstrate the lack of value that children are assigned, still today, in Western culture.

Jesus's heart for children, as illustrated in this story, shows that American society has the social value of children contorted and entirely upside down.

The Bible says that Jesus was "indignant"—a nice biblical term that covers up the raw truth that Jesus was downright mad at how the disciples were trying to shoo the little ones away. Rather than relegating children to the bottom of the social pecking order, Jesus stated very clearly that no one can enter the Kingdom of God without imitating the nature and behavior of children. They are not "afterthoughts" but spiritual models to be emulated. What is it about children that Jesus finds so appealing in terms of spiritual qualities? Is it the fact that they generally trust those who provide for them and are entirely dependent on the grace of another? Is it the fact that they know how to play and enjoy life rather than working so hard all the time to try to attain a heightened level of personal accomplishment or even heaven itself? Is it the fact that they are emotionally honest, in their laughter and in their tears? I think the answer includes all of the above.

The end of the story finds the children being hugged by Jesus and no doubt being held in his lap. He laid his hands on them to bless them with all of the riches He had been given by His heavenly Father. Can you think of a more tender scene in all of the Scripture than this? Isn't it amazing and saddening that we can treat children so miserably sometimes when Father God Himself calls us *His* children—the relationship He chose to define and illustrate who we are in Christ. Isaiah 11:6 tells us that "a little child will lead them"—meaning that the whole created order will be led by a child—the Child-Savior Jesus and the life lessons learned through observing the beauty of children. Truly, let it be so!

## PRAYER

*Heavenly Father, we love being Your children. Keep us from minimizing the importance of children and even hurting them by our words or our actions. Cause us to observe the children around us, care for them, and learn from them. In Jesus's name, amen.*

# THE SOUND OF SILENCE

*After he had dismissed [the crowds],*
*[Jesus]went up on a mountainside by himself to pray.*
*Later that night, He was there alone.*

MATTHEW 14:23

The world is full of noise. I remember the lyrics to a song written and recorded in 1966 by Fred Neil called "Everybody's Talkin": "Everybody's talking at me. I don't hear a word they're saying." Ever feel that way? And then we compound the decibel level with our high-tech toys—iPods, smart phones, bluetooth this, and bluetooth that. Everywhere I go on campus, I see people with buds in their ears and eyes fixated on phones. I am just as guilty as the next person. We get in our cars and turn on our radios because that's what we do, listening to nonstop, often trivial political commentary, sports talk, or music. Sometimes I think it is hard for the Lord to even get a word in edgewise to those of us who really want to hear what He has to say to us. What are we to do with the "crowds" comprised of all these voices?

If you do a commentary search on the word "crowds," you will find that, almost all of the time, Jesus had compassion on large groups of people. Jesus saw the pain and brokenness of each individual who needed His healing touch. Nonetheless, the Gospel writer and disciple Matthew noted that, after miraculously feeding five thousand people near Capernaum, Jesus "dismissed" the crowd and then went up on a mountainside alone to pray. Matthew made a point of writing that Jesus was there alone; His disciples were already in a boat on the Sea of Galilee headed to the other side of the lake (Matthew 14:22–23). I am certain that Jesus was tired from a long day of ministry and needed solitude—just Him and His Heavenly Father. The "push and pull" of serving so many people, listening to their questions, and carrying their burdens had no doubt taxed both Jesus's physical and emotional resources. Jesus dismissed the crowd so that He could listen to His Father. We should do the same.

Let's be honest. Some of us are afraid to be alone. And even when we are by ourselves, the noise continues—voices of self-doubt, guilt, shame, or fear. We choose to live in a world of superficial sound because it is just too frightening or uncomfortable for us to experience solitude. Noise helps us to take our minds off what the Lord might actually want to draw attention to in our lives. This feels safer, less vulnerable for us. Honestly, we need to be away from the crowds so that we will realize our dependence on the Lord and our absolute weakness apart from Him. Beyond that, time apart with the Lord allows Him to clarify the high purpose He has for our lives as subjects in the Kingdom of God. If Jesus needed the time alone, we most certainly do.

What does this look like? I'm sure it is different for each one of us. Jesus told His disciples to "go into your room, close the door and pray" (Matthew 6:6). And that would work—but there are other ways to find the solitude that we so desperately need in this noisy world. I actually find myself able to think and sense what the Lord might be saying to me when I mow the lawn. Some people find solitude in the shower, through an early morning or late evening walk, or just sitting in a car for a few extra minutes with the radio off. In Mark 4:34, we read that, when Jesus "was alone with his own disciples, he explained everything." Anyone want to sign up for that experience? We will often need to be alone to hear the voice of the Lord clearly and receive the explanations He would like to offer to us.

PRAYER

*Heavenly Father, it does seem as though everybody's talking at us, so much so that we don't hear a word You are saying. Help us to take whatever steps we need to be alone with You. We don't want to turn our backs on a needy world—and we don't think You want us to do that, either. But we can be more like You with others if we will spend some time apart, and quiet, with You alone. Allow us to experience the sort of intimacy that we would know if we were the only person in the universe with You; You love each one of us with that sort of unique and profound power. In Jesus's name, amen.*

# CLOSE TO HOME

# UNSUNG HEROES

*"My grace is sufficient for you, for my power
is made perfect in weakness."*

2 CORINTHIANS 12:9

When I pray, I start by talking through with the Lord the things for which I am most thankful. Topping my gratitude list are the "heroes" God has allowed me to come to know through almost 64 years of life. These "heroes" are almost never famous people by worldly standards, but they show me Jesus in the way they speak, the way they think, and the way they live. At the head of the line of my heroes is my wife, Janet.

Janet has faced and continues to face her share of adversity in life. She contracted Lyme Disease when she was young, which means that she faces physical limitations that most people don't understand and that can prevent some people from pursuing activities as easily as they would wish. But that hasn't stopped my wife. She is a respected fourth-grade teacher, a veteran instructor teaching a class of gifted and talented students. She raised her two little boys all alone for a number of years, while also going to school and working, before I ever met her. And through it all, both in good and in tough times, Janet held on to the Lord as He held on to her. What have I learned from my wife?

*Living in an authentic, sincere fashion attracts others and glorifies the Lord.* When I met Janet initially, what impressed me most was how "real" she was. There is nothing fake about Janet—no masks, no disguise. Of all of the ways that we can live, I think authenticity is a trait that pleases the Lord more than almost anything else. He can work with us best if we are honest with ourselves and with others. Sometimes Janet is too hard on herself, which can be a problem for people without guile, but, on the other hand, the Lord doesn't have to waste time scraping away deceit if we live sincerely before Him. Want to know how much the Lord values authenticity? He gave the prophet Jeremiah these instructions: "Go up and down the streets of Jerusalem, look around and consider, search through her squares. If you can find but one person who deals honestly and seeks the truth, I will forgive this city" (Jeremiah 5:1). Let's lay aside the facade we wrap around ourselves to impress or influence others—or even God.

*It is important to laugh.* Janet often says that she felt as though one of the assignments God gave her when we got married was to get me to laugh. I have always been a more serious person than many others—no doubt more serious than I needed to be. Janet walks out Proverbs 31:25: "She is clothed with strength and dignity; she can laugh at the days to come." My wife makes me laugh and encourages me in the process. And why can she laugh? Because her Maker laughs as well. At the birth of Isaac, his mother, Sarah, declared that God had brought her laughter. King Solomon himself affirmed that "a cheerful heart is good medicine" (Proverbs 17:22). Because the Lord is on His throne, in control, life's circumstances are never quite as bad as they may seem. In fact, what we see around us might just deserve a good laugh.

*Trust is essential to a healthy relationship.* Because she has been the victim of betrayal on more than one occasion, my wife prioritizes trust in her relationships. I believe she values trust more than almost any other ingredient of human interaction. In his first letter to Timothy, the apostle Paul commanded that women in the early Christian churches were to be "worthy of respect, not malicious talkers but temperate and trustworthy in everything" (3:11). Can people trust us to be loyal and gracious toward them? Do we keep our word and prove ourselves trustworthy? Let's pray that the Lord will help us all to live this way.

Finally, *we are braver and stronger than we could ever imagine.* When Janet was four months pregnant with her youngest son, Benjamin, a time that should have been of great happiness for a couple, her first marriage ended. Alex was four at the time. Then, when Benjamin was born, he had a rare heart condition that required open-heart surgery almost immediately and nearly cost him his life. Things seemed to be going from awful to the worst imaginable. Her faith was challenged at points, but Janet clung tenaciously to the Lord in the darkest hours. Janet's experiences proved the timeless spiritual truth that God's grace keeps us where His will leads us. Janet would be the first to tell you that she felt very weak through all of these trials, but that weakness displayed the power of the Lord most majestically. We are strong in His strength; we overcome through the Cross!

## P R A Y E R

*Heavenly Father, we thank You for the "heroes" You bring into our lives to love us and to teach us about Your love. Help us all to live authentically, to laugh often, to earn the trust of others, and to depend upon You and Your grace at all times. We need You desperately! In Jesus's name, amen.*

# KNOWING GOD

*Adam knew Eve his wife; and she conceived.*

GENESIS 4:1, KJV

M y wife, Janet, is my best friend and my strongest supporter in ministry. This devotional selection originated in the following words that she shared with me: "Sometimes we get so focused on trying to 'see' Jesus work in our lives that we don't recognize our need to get to 'know' Him. In other words, we want to trust Him by observing surface things about His work in our lives without truly knowing Him deeply. All of this begs two questions: Who is He, really? and How do I get to know Him?"

Knowing the Lord is truly at the crux of what it means to be a Jesus follower. In the first half of the Western civilization history survey course that I teach at Purdue University Fort Wayne, I actually have the opportunity to explain to my students what "knowing" the Lord meant to the Hebrew mind. In the book of Genesis, chapter 4, verse 1, you will read, in some of the earlier English translations like the King James Version, that Adam "knew" Eve and that she bore a son, whom the couple named Cain. The Hebrew word translated "knew" is *yada*, and it obviously implies sexual intercourse. So, to the ancient Israelite, to know someone meant to know him or her in relational intimacy. "Knowing" to the Greek mind, on the other hand, meant accumulating intellectual facts—quite different from the scriptural perspective. Biblically, to know means to relate intimately. That is what is required to truly know Jesus. We don't need to make a list of what He has done for us—or of what we perceive he has not done for us. We need to spend time with Him every day on a level at which our heart (mind, emotions, will, and spirit) is entirely engaged by His ever-present Spirit.

Which is true for you—what you see and experience around you or what you read in the Scripture? The answer to this question will determine what you know about the Lord. If it is what you observe and experience, you will draw conclusions about the Lord that are mistaken and that will lead you to doubt His goodness and His power. If what you "know" (through relational intimacy) about the Lord is what the Holy Spirit teaches you, however, while you are reading the Word of God, then your understanding of the Lord will be true and constant, no matter what is going on around you. Yes, there will be times when life experiences confirm what you read in the Bible. But that reaffirmation cannot be the proof for you that the Bible is true. We can know that the Lord is Who the Bible says He is (by faith) whether or not what we see bears that out.

## PRAYER

*Heavenly Father, we want to grow in our knowledge of You. In other words, we want to become more intimate in our relationship with You. Would You help us? We want to go beyond just sight to a faith relationship with You and a greater understanding of You as You reveal Yourself in Your Word. Thank You that You are even more eager to produce this knowledge in us than we ourselves are to receive it. Help us to trust You even when everything that we see around us seems to question Your mercy and Your grace. In Jesus's name, amen.*

# BE SILENT AND STILL

*The LORD is in his holy temple;*
*let all the earth be silent before him.*

HABAKKUK 2:20

I married into a wonderful family of Tennesseans back in 1997. Most of the extended family of my wife, Janet, still live in Knoxville, Tennessee, and we try to spend at least one week each summer with them. A favorite vacation spot when we join them is Fall Creek Falls State Park in Spencer, Tennessee. Janet grew up vacationing in this state park as a little girl each summer, so the place holds dear memories for her. My wife's family is a bike-riding clan, so, when we got married, I purchased a bike to join in on the fun. One summer about four years ago, we biked through this park every day, dodging thunderstorms and having a great time. One day, we biked for 13 miles around a gorge with many uphill climbs along the way—great exercise but hard on my 59-year-old legs! When I wasn't struggling to catch my breath, I was overwhelmed by the tranquility, beauty, and stillness of the forest paths we rode!

Meanwhile, whenever I checked the news feed on my cell phone, I read about violence and turmoil in yet another part of the world. 2016 included a summer of terrible tragedy—Orlando, Minnesota, Louisiana, Dallas, and other situations that did not achieve the notoriety to gain national attention. 2020 has brought more of the same. How do we reconcile a world of beauty and peace with the terrible things people do to each other? How can the same God be Lord over these contrasting "worlds?" I'm thinking that maybe what I saw in that Tennessee state park is a pattern for the way God intends the world to be, while what we see in the news is the inevitable result of human beings trying to take matters into their own hands for some end, evil or otherwise. When will we learn that there is a God—and that we aren't Him? When will we imitate the waterfalls I saw during that week? The water pours itself out, always going lower, bringing refreshment wherever it goes. Likewise, we can seek to serve others humbly and self-sacrificially. When will we learn to just be still and know that He is God? (Psalm 46:10)

In the stillness of those forest paths, I heard the whisper of His voice. The trick is to practice peace and tranquility in our day-to-day living in order to continue to hear Him in a world gone mad with sinful, selfish hatred and even violent insanity. It will take discipline to hear the Lord above all the hateful din of this world—but we will be larger, kinder, and more compassionate people if we make the sacrifice to take our place quietly at the feet of our heavenly Father. In that position, we can and must speak up for the victims of injustice and discrimination.

In a world of political upheaval and military conquest, a world not that much different from ours, the prophet Habakkuk spoke the words printed at the beginning of this devotion. Habakkuk was testifying that, even when the world seems to be falling apart and there is no apparent sense to it all, the Lord is still on the throne. He is in complete control despite appearances. If I accept that truth, there is only one response that is demanded of me—stop talking, stop doing, stop fretting, stop feuding, and just be still, yielded and ready to listen. Adopt the posture of the quiet mountain stream—keep flowing from your Source to the place He intends you to go (ultimately home with Him), refreshing others all along the way. Stillness is an act of adoration and worship. Stillness says, "You have this, Lord, and you don't need my help." Stillness shows a watching world that there is a God Who loves us, a God Whom we can trust without hesitation.

## PRAYER

*Heavenly Father, thank You for the beauty of Your creation. Help us to learn a lesson of quietness, trust, and stillness from the natural world around us. Comfort those in turmoil this week, and meet them with Your Presence so that they can rest and find peace. You are an awesome, majestic God and we worship You! In Jesus's name, amen.*

# MAKE ME MORE LIKE MY DOG

*You are my hiding place; you will protect me from trouble
and surround me with songs of deliverance.*
PSALM 32:7

Five years ago, our family faced a deep personal loss, hurtful but not uncommon. We had to put our little Bichon Frise dog, Simon, to sleep due to a host of physical problems from which he was not going to recover. He was clearly hurting, but, nevertheless, this was one of the hardest decisions we have ever had to make in our lives. Simon lived with us for 15 ½ years. At that time, Janet and I had been married for 18 years—so Simon had been with us for about as long as our family had existed. We brought him home at seven weeks old. The first night he was with us, he was suffering from separation anxiety from his mother, crying and barking most of the night. Finally, I just came downstairs with my pillow, lay on the living room floor next to his cage, and slipped my finger in through the bars. This little puppy sucked on my finger most of the night. All came full circle when we spent several of the last few nights of his life staying near him, sleeping on the couch downstairs, just to be sure he wasn't suffering.

Our minds were flooded with memories as we walked through the sadness of the loss of our dog. One of the most therapeutic ways to deal with grief, whether it is for a person or a pet, is to reflect on these recollections, wipe away a tear or two, and savor a smile provoked by the memory. I am a dog lover, and I will tell you that I admire them in many ways. Thinking about our little dog's life has provided examples that are worthy of imitation. I would like to describe a few of those examples in this and the next devotion.

*Simon was protective and brave.* Many years ago, a guy broke into our house during the night. We were asleep upstairs in our bedrooms, and Simon was in his usual place in the little crate next to my desk. His cage was

70

out of sight of the sliding glass door through which the intruder entered. We had no home alarm system at this point, and, of course, the situation was very dangerous. Simon heard the prowler moving around the room and began to bark loudly and persistently. I was roused from sleep and, after a few minutes, came downstairs to see what the dog was so excited about. By then, the burglar had beaten a quick retreat after taking a few things close at hand. There is no telling what could have happened to us had Simon not sounded the alarm. Of course, he did not know that he was being protective or brave; he was just being a dog. But I wish I were more like that—instinctively protecting others who are vulnerable, no matter the cost or danger to myself. If I were, I would be imitating our Lord Himself. "You are my hiding place; you will protect me from trouble and surround me with songs [barking] of deliverance" (Psalm 32:7). To take the pressure off Simon, we installed a security system shortly after the burglary.

## PRAYER

*Heavenly Father, You teach us in so many, and often unexpected, ways. Thank you for both the affection and the instruction You offered us through our little dog. Keep us alert and aware of the lessons You have sprinkled along our way as we walk through each day. In Jesus's name, amen.*

# MORE WAYS I WISH I WERE
# LIKE MY DOG

*"The wind blows wherever it pleases. You hear its sound,
but you cannot tell where it comes from or where it is going.
So it is with everyone born of the Spirit."*

JOHN 3:8

Simon *was always thrilled to see us.* We kept our dog in a little crate next to my desk in the family room when we were away. The door to the garage was just a few feet from his "safe place." Whenever we opened the garage door to pull the car in, we could hear Simon barking already. We would come into the house and open the little door of his crate, and he would run around from one to the other of us, tail wagging. I always knew that, even if everyone else in the family (or the world) were exasperated with me, that little dog would still be happy to see me. His affection was unqualified—not based on my appearance, my failures, my issues, or my behavior. I wish I were more like that—happy to see people, delighted in their presence, gracious in my acceptance of them, looking for the good in them. Love "does not dishonor others, it is not self-seeking, it is not easily angered, it keeps no record of wrongs" (1 Corinthians 13:5).

Simon *became more and more obedient over time.* Our little dog was very smart from the beginning, but he didn't mind very well at first. I can't tell you the number of times we had to drive all over the neighborhood looking for him after he had darted out our front door. People we didn't even know who lived several streets away would bring him home, telling us that they had found him standing in their yard. We realized that Simon needed obedience training, so we took him to classes while he was still quite young. The first night of class was a disaster. All of the other dogs were reasonably well behaved, while our little Bichon was running from one dog to the next, smelling them and causing a commotion. The instructor told us that we might have to use a spiked collar for training purposes.

However, by the end of the class sessions, Simon was the star pupil. He was sitting, lying down, and following us on our left heel all through hand commands. (We never could get the fetch command right, however; he would love to play ball and then drop it five to six feet away from our feet to make us go get it.) I wish I were more like this—learning to be increasingly faithful without any thought of disobeying my Master. I want a heart that instinctively follows the Lord without any inclination to wander away—or at least a heart that is moving in that direction more and more every day. "Follow my decrees and be careful to obey my laws, and you will live safely in the land" (Leviticus 25:18).

Simon *loved to sniff the wind.* The strongest of the five senses in a dog is that of smell, and they love to stick their faces out of car windows and sniff the wind. Simon was the same way. Even though he was a tiny dog, never weighing much more than ten pounds, he would sometimes pull himself up on his hind legs, stick his nose out the passenger window while I was driving him to the groomer or to the veterinarian, and push his snout out into the breeze. Even when he walked out into our backyard, I would watch him pause, stand still, and sniff when a gust of wind passed by him. I wish I were more like that—sniffing the wind of the Holy Spirit to see which direction the Spirit was moving in my life. I would like to be led by that Spirit more easily, constantly testing the spiritual breeze to see where and how the Lord is at work around me.

P R A Y E R

*Heavenly Father, we miss our little dog. We believe that You take care of all creation, all living things, because You are a good and compassionate God. Be near to all those who are grieving today, whether they have lost a pet, a family member, a friend, or perhaps suffered the loss of a relationship, job, or opportunity. Help us to be kind and loving to all of your creation. And help us to be more like our dogs. In Jesus's name, amen.*

# MATTERS
## OF THE HEART

# A HEALTHY HEART

*I trust in your unfailing love;*
*my heart rejoices in your salvation.*

PSALM 13:5

Did you know that the word translated "heart" in the English appears almost twice as often in the Old Testament book of Psalms than in any other book of the Bible? The word is mentioned 725 times throughout the Scripture and appears 127 times in Psalms. I guess I am not surprised by this fact, in that the book of Psalms is the Bible's songbook—and songs have a special impact on the proverbial "heart" or seat of our emotions. While emotions do not carry the weight of any love relationship, human or divine (our will to love does that), they nonetheless motivate, encourage, and inspire us to nurture the love relationships into which we have entered. That is why David sang in Psalm 37, encouraging us to "take delight in the LORD, and he will give you the desires of your heart" (verse 4). If you are delighting in the Lord in the first place, then that delight becomes the desire of your heart first and foremost.

It is that delight in the Lord which I believe to be the measure of the health of our relationship with the Lord. The measurement is not how much I pray, nor how often I read the Bible or go to church—or anything else I do, for that matter. The measure of the health of any relationship is the state of our heart in the midst of it. A better question than "Are you praying?" is "Do you want to pray?" These aren't the same questions at all—I could be praying for a whole host of reasons (duty, fear, habit, and so on) that might have nothing to do with whether my heart is sincerely in it. And only God and I can know the state of my heart. That is why we should always try to avoid assessing the state of someone else's relationship with the Lord. In the first place, we aren't supposed to judge—and in the second place, we can't anyway.

*Heavenly Father, thank You for the opportunity to love You. We know that we have that privilege only because You first loved us. We want to become better lovers of You and of each other this week. Create in us a clean heart, O Lord, and renew a right spirit in us all week long. In Jesus's name, amen.*

# AN UNDIVIDED HEART

*Teach me your way, Lord, that I may rely on*
*your faithfulness; give me an undivided heart,*
*that I may fear your name. I will praise you, Lord my God,*
*with all my heart; I will glorify your name forever.*

PSALM 86:11–12

Often people talk about the heart as more than just a bodily organ. How do we understand that? What the Bible calls the "heart" is, practically speaking, most realistically associated with certain parts of our brain. The right side of the brain is the creative, emotional part, while the left side is often associated with our cognitive abilities. When we talk about our heart as the seat of our emotions, our will, our desires, and so on, we know that we aren't literally talking about the muscle in our chest that pumps blood. Still, the Scripture addresses the importance of the orientation of our hearts when it comes to being a follower of Christ.

The fascinating aspect of how the poetry in the book of Psalms is written is that often the first part of a verse reflects or parallels what is written in the second half. So, in the verse above, being taught the way of the Lord defines for us what the writer means by having an "undivided heart." Walking in the truth of God's Word means learning to trust and not waver in our commitment to the Lord and His ways. Nothing is worse in the world than being torn between believing and doubting, desiring, and avoiding.

And yet some of us live our lives that way. We want to be followers of the Lord, but only to the degree that it is convenient and doesn't interfere with our desires and our plans. We live our spiritual lives "on the fence"; we have divided our lives into compartments, and the Lord gets our Sunday morning compartment, perhaps along with some weekday church-related activities or commitments. The rest belongs to us. The psalmist in this verse realizes both the futility and the emptiness that this sort of life will yield. An "undivided," fully committed heart (life) "fears" God's name—that is, the fully committed life reverences and trusts Who God is and the richness of His character.

The word *integrity* comes from the root word *integer*. We know from our study of basic mathematics that an integer is a whole number that cannot be divided. Likewise, a person who lives with integrity lives without hypocrisy; her motives and actions cannot be divided into what is true and what is not true. Being lukewarm in our commitment to the Lord is not satisfying and is actually steadily discouraging. So, let's begin today with a fresh prayer to live our lives one hundred percent for the Lord—whatever that costs us and whatever sacrifices need to be made right away. We will be happier, and the Lord will be glorified by how we are living.

## P R A Y E R

*Heavenly Father, give us all undivided hearts so that we might fear Your name and walk in Your truth. Show us what Your truth is, no matter how painful applying that truth might be to us personally, and give us the desire to honor that truth with our words, actions, thoughts, desires, and relationships. Thank You that Your truth truly does set us free. In Jesus's name, amen.*

# ETERNITY IN OUR HEARTS

*He has made everything beautiful in its time.*
*He has also set eternity in the human heart; yet no one*
*can fathom what God has done from beginning to end.*

ECCLESIASTES 3:11

Ecclesiastes is a much darker, more pessimistic book than Proverbs. Though both were written by King Solomon of Israel, perhaps Ecclesiastes represents the reflections of a king who has become more cynical in later life. First Kings 11:4 records the following failure of an older Solomon: "As Solomon grew old, his wives turned his heart after other gods, and his heart was not fully devoted to the LORD his God, as the heart of David his father had been." Maybe Solomon's negativity and sense of futility, on full display in Ecclesiastes, stemmed from the fact that his walk with the Lord was becoming more shaky and compromised.

Regardless, there are some wonderful words of wisdom found in the book of Ecclesiastes. First, in the verse referenced above, we read that God makes everything beautiful in its time. The problem, the apparent disconnect from reality as we know it, with this declaration is that life serves up some truly ugly and painful circumstances that we have to navigate. We learn that a loved one has cancer. Someone we trusted hurts us badly, perhaps damaging or destroying our relationship. We experience a financial loss that completely alters our fortunes. How can any of this be made beautiful? Do I believe that God causes any of this to happen to get our attention? No, I do not. We live in a world corrupted by the sin of our own human making. But do I believe that the Lord can make beauty emerge from the ashes of death and destruction? Yes, I do. Death, sickness, brokenness, and pain are parts of life because humankind has strayed from and rebelled against the Lord. But God can and will redeem these blights, in their time, and produce from them something beautiful. We just need to watch for it. It may take time for the beauty to emerge, but God has promised here to create it.

Another difficult reality that many of us face is that we have loved ones who have turned their backs on God. Some are just indifferent to the Lord, while others are truly hostile toward the idea of following Him. It can be discouraging to pray for someone we love for years and to see no sign that they are drawing closer to Jesus. Ecclesiastes 3:11 encourages us, however, because God has put eternity into the hearts of all people He has created— and that means all of us, even the loved one who has no apparent interest in Him. What this means to me is that, down deep inside, in our hearts, we all know that God created us for more than just this life. That is why someone who is not following the Lord, if he or she is honest, will admit that their life feels empty and unfulfilled. That very feeling of meaninglessness (a theme that Solomon repeats over and over in the book of Ecclesiastes) can be used by God to drive our loved ones right back to Him. We also know that the Lord is relentlessly pursuing all people with a love that has no quit in it. The combination of eternity implanted within each heart, along with the irrepressible, loving pursuit of the eternal One outside each heart means that we should never give up on anyone finally surrendering their lives to the Lord.

## PRAYER

*Heavenly Father, thank You that You make everything, the good and the bad, the joyous and the sorrowful, beautiful at just the right time. Please help us to be patient and to trust You in this process. We pray today for those people we know who have walked away from You for one reason or another. Would You please stir up that sense of eternity in their hearts and remind them that You love them more than they can possibly imagine? In Jesus's name, amen.*

# WAITING ON GOD'S TIME

*"Let both grow together until the harvest."*
MATTHEW 13:30

I learned many lessons about life and ministry during the course of serving college-age youth for 23 years. Most of the knowledge was acquired through trial and error—with a high incidence of the error part. One thing I noticed in myself and others was the natural tendency to want to sort out someone else's life the moment they start having troubles or seem to be wandering off the straight and narrow path. Sadly, I think this is a natural impulse that is a part of our sinful nature—that desire to control the lives of others, supposedly, at least from our perspective, for "their own good." What I have learned is that in our rush to judge the failings and misconduct of others, and to do something about the problem if we are in a position of leadership or relationship, we are pre-emptively inserting ourselves into a role that is best occupied by God the Holy Spirit. By assuming that place, we can interrupt the work the Lord is trying to do in that other person's life, while damaging our relationship with the person in the process.

The Gospel writer Matthew recorded a story Jesus told his followers that illustrated this principle. Beginning in verse 24 of Matthew 13, the Lord described a man who owned a field. Naturally, he sowed only good seed in his field, but one day his servants found weeds growing in the midst of the early sprouts of wheat. Sharing the news with their master, the servants offered to pull up the weeds immediately. Wisely, the master acknowledged that the weeds were the work of an enemy but cautioned those who worked for him not to be too eager to eradicate them. Rather, he instructed the servants to hold off until the wheat and the weeds had grown to the point that they could be easily differentiated and separated. In that way, as few of the healthy wheat plants as possible would be uprooted.

We don't know with any great depth of knowledge what is behind some of the trials and struggles others experience. We may think we do, but the truth is that only the Lord fully understands each situation. The truth of this reality is recorded six chapters earlier in Matthew through a question Jesus poses in His Sermon on the Mount: "Why do you look at the speck of sawdust in your brother's eye and pay no attention to the plank in your own eye?" (Matthew 7:3). How can we possibly believe that we can see the other guy's speck when a large plank is obscuring our own vision? The Lord alone knows the appointed time when the struggle will come to a head and a person will be ready to release the weeds that the enemy has sown into their life. I'm not saying that we should ignore all circumstances when a person is clearly hurting themselves or others through sinful behavior, but I think that too often we err on the side of jumping in prematurely to "solve" other people's problems when maybe we should just wait. We should do what the servants did in Jesus's story. We should ask the Master when it is time to intervene and be willing to wait beyond our level of comfort or felt need to exert control if the Holy Spirit holds us back. That way we won't obstruct or distract from how the Lord may already be working in a less blatant but more powerful manner. We should show to others the same grace and kindness the Lord has shown to us.

## PRAYER

*Heavenly Father, this is a hard line to draw. When do you want us to speak into the lives of those whom the enemy is attacking? When do you want us to wait and trust that You are working in an unseen, life-transforming way? Please make that clear to us. Help us to be more concerned about the planks blocking our own vision than the specks we perceive affecting others' sight. In Jesus's name, amen.*

# MY OWN FAITH

*"My ears had heard of you but now my eyes have seen you."*
JOB 42:5

Many people walk through life without a definitive relationship with the Lord. They may know that their parents, or spouse, or good friends have what seems to be a genuine relationship with God. And some of them base their faith on the faith demonstrated by these people. But that second-hand spirituality won't sustain us in the challenging, painful trials we all face if we live any length of time. Like Job, I may have heard about the Lord from others, but nothing short of seeing Him alive and active in my own life will help me stay true to Him when I feel alone or desperate.

I wish there were some other way of seeing the Lord, of truly encountering Him without suffering, but there doesn't seem to be. If you have read the book of Job, you know that this man, apparently godly and faithful in every way, loses everything. His children die, his possessions are destroyed, and his friends turn on him, encouraging him to admit to sins he has not committed against the Lord. Many people struggle with this Old Testament story because it seems unfair and arbitrary. But the bottom line is that we all suffer and struggle, whether or not we "deserve" to. It is how we deal with that suffering that determines whether we "see" the Lord. When all is going well, it is easy to forget about the Lord and focus our attention on ourselves. But when life if falling apart, we are more likely to look in God's direction for help or answers. Job's response to his trials is not always pretty; he gets to the point at which he is wishing he were dead (or had never been born), mad at his friends, and very mad at God. The main point is, Job was honest with God in his feelings. He let God have it. And then, toward the end of the book, God let Job have it. They had a very real encounter—and it wouldn't be a stretch to imagine some yelling going on during the conversation. This was an honest, life-changing moment for Job—no pretense, no fake religious positivity, no concern about what others thought.

Maybe you or I need to have it out with God today. We need to be honest in our feelings of frustration—or maybe our feelings of dependence and passion. If we are bitter against God or others because of the way we have been treated in the past, let's recognize that and admit it. It is time for us not just to hear about God but to see Him authentically encountering us where we are. And that won't happen unless we honestly and independently engage Him in prayer, in His Word, by the Spirit. I don't think there is anything overly mystical about the encounter I am describing; it is simply an encounter born of faith—faith that God exists, that He loves me more than I can imagine, and that He wants me to surrender every area of my life to Him. If we meet the Lord on these terms, He will speak to us in some recognizable way as He did to Job, reaffirming what we read in the Bible and applying it uniquely and intimately to our lives. Then we can say that we have not just heard about the Lord from others but have seen Him for ourselves. We have a personal story of faith to tell—and we, like Job, will never be the same.

## PRAYER

*Heavenly Father, thank You that You helped Job, and so many others through time, remain faithful to You during the hard times. Would You do that for us when we need You to? Help us to be honest with ourselves rather than playing religious games or worrying about what others think about us. Make our relationship with You genuine, unique, and life-sustaining. In Jesus's name, amen.*

# A PATTERN
## OF PRAYER

# GETTING TO JESUS

*When the Sabbath was over, Mary Magdalene,*
*Mary the mother of James, and Salome bought spices so that*
*they might go to anoint Jesus' body. Very early on the first*
*day of the week, just after sunrise, they were on their way*
*to the tomb and they asked each other, "Who will roll the*
*stone away from the entrance of the tomb?"*

MARK 16:1–3

I find the question that these women asked each other in this passage to be very interesting—and a little bit odd. The Bible tells us that the stone in front of Jesus's tomb was very large, and the Gospel of Matthew mentions that these women had witnessed Joseph of Arimathea, the owner of the tomb, placing Jesus's body in the tomb and rolling the stone into place. Why would these women buy spices to anoint Jesus's body and then strike off for the burial location if they could not actually get to Jesus's corpse to accomplish their mission? Wouldn't you think first, "Wait a minute, we can't get to his body to do what we want to do. The stone is in the way, and it is too heavy for us to move. So, I guess we might as well give up on our idea of anointing the body. Why bother?" This would be the logical train of thought. It seems strange that the women would actually walk to the tomb without having their question answered.

The only explanation I can come up with for the fact that they actually struck out for the tomb with their query unanswered is that they were bound and determined to get to Jesus in order to worship Him through the act of anointing. They loved the Lord and were passionate to serve Him even after He had died. Remember, too, that, at this point they had no clear idea that He would rise again. These women just wanted to be with Jesus no matter what; they had to get to Him. And they were not going to allow a big boulder, or their difficult question, or any other obstacle, for that matter, to keep them from being with Jesus.

Many of us find ourselves at times in the same situation these women faced. There is some major barrier, some huge stone that is keeping us from being in relationship with Jesus. Maybe it is a major sin or failure—and all of the guilt that comes with it. Maybe it is the doubt that flows out of circumstances that simply seem impossible to overcome. Maybe it is the fear that the Lord has left me or that He is not hearing my cries for help. Maybe it is a multitude of fears or anxieties that leave us with nothing but weariness and turmoil in our souls. Maybe it is the hurt, disappointment, sadness, and pain that come with the betrayal of a friend or family member. Maybe it is the disillusionment of serving the Lord faithfully but feeling as though that service is either insignificant or inconsequential. Or maybe it is something else that I haven't articulated. But whatever it is, it is keeping you from Jesus. And the one question we have is, "Who will roll the stone away for us so that we can be with Jesus?"

The answer to the question of the women, and to our question as well, was shockingly and wonderfully apparent when the ladies reached the tomb. Mark explains in verse 4 of chapter 16 that, when they looked up, the stone had been rolled away. The women had been looking down, perhaps out of despair, dread, or the disappointment that had come when Jesus's crucifixion shattered their hopes for a Messiah and His kingdom. Then they looked up and ultimately realized the answer to their question: the Lord Himself had rolled the stone away. Jesus did what was necessary for these women to get to Him. But what He did for them was more than they had hoped or expected. A corpse to anoint was gone; a living Lord was their new reality.

If you are trying to get to Jesus today and there is something in the way, look up. Look up and see that, in His way and in His timing, the Lord will remove that stone or barrier that is keeping you from being in His presence with peace and joy. He will do it—you don't have to do anything to make it happen. And when that boulder-sized blockage is removed, you will find that Jesus is more than you had ever imagined Him to be. He is a living Lord who will surprise you, amaze you, rescue you, and love you in ways beyond your understanding.

## PRAYER

*Heavenly Father, we so want to be with You. We are passionate to be in Your Presence and to live there day by day. If there is anything keeping us from living fully in the Presence of Your Spirit, would You get rid of that big stone for us? Roll it away, Lord, so that we can see and experience the full power and majesty of our risen King. It is in His name that we pray, amen.*

# RESPONDING TO
# ROCK-THROWERS

*"Leave him alone; let him curse, for the LORD has told him to. It may be that the LORD will look upon my misery and restore to me his covenant blessing instead of his curse today."*

2 SAMUEL 16:11–12

There is a fascinating, and frankly, a bit odd, story in the Old Testament book of 2 Samuel, chapter 16. King David was forced to flee the capital city of Jerusalem when his son Absalom carried out a rebellion against his rule. As David fled the city, a man by the name of Shimei, a member of the same clan as David's predecessor, King Saul, began to pelt David and his officials with stones, cursing the king as well. Shimei shouted insults at David and repeatedly called him a murderer. One of David's generals, Abishai, took offense at what Shimei was doing, calling him a dead dog and offering to cut off his head. David rebuked Abishai for the violence of his threat. David's response, quoted above, is worthy of our consideration. David and his entourage journeyed along the road, while Shimei continued to bombard David and his party with rocks and insults. The story ended with King David arriving at his destination exhausted—no wonder!

I am often more tempted to pursue the response of Abishai than that of David. Whenever I am insulted or people say hurtful things about me, I want to retaliate, and I will even think long and hard about what I can do to defend myself from the unfairness of what is being asserted about me. Maybe you, too? I believe, however, that the path of wisdom stretches out in front of David's words. Interestingly, David admonished Abishai, telling him that the Lord had told Shimei to curse him. I am not sure how David knew that, but at least it is obvious that the Lord was allowing this man to insult King David. Likewise, when others speak ill of us, there can be no disagreement that the Lord is allowing it. And if the Lord is allowing it, as David recognized, the Lord can also produce something of benefit for the target of the insult—as hard as that may be to believe and accept. What could that benefit possibly be?

In the first place, there could easily be some truth for us to learn from the harsh words spoken about us if we will not take offense to the point that we refuse to listen and consider what is being said. In the case of David, *he was a murderer*. He had admitted that himself to the prophet Nathan four chapters earlier in 2 Samuel. Shimei called David a scoundrel who had shed blood—all of that was true. Perhaps what others say about us negatively might also contain a grain, or several grains, of truth. We could really benefit from a moment of honesty and humility in recognizing this reality. Perhaps listening and reflecting will save us from failure and sin at future points in time.

Second, David's response put the focus right where it belonged—on himself and not on Shimei. I know that, when I am criticized or judged, especially when I feel that the negative assumptions about me are unjustified, I want to judge and condemn the source of the accusations against me. That instinct is wrong. At the end of the day, I need to decide to whom I will turn to be my defender—me or the Lord. Again, Jesus established the model. In his prophecy of the atoning death of Jesus, the Lamb of God, Isaiah declared, "He was oppressed and afflicted, yet He did not open His mouth" (Isaiah 53:7). Before the accusations of the Sanhedrin, and even Pontius Pilate himself, Jesus chose not to say a word in His own defense. Why? Because He trusted His heavenly Father to provide the necessary protection. And if this life is ultimately more about Jesus than it is about me, then my reputation or what others say about me is not of that great a consequence anyway. As Peter wrote in his first letter, "When they hurled their insults at him [Jesus], he did not retaliate; when he suffered, he made no threats. Instead, he entrusted himself to him who judges justly" (1 Peter 2:23).

## PRAYER

*Heavenly Father, it is hard when we are the target of unkind words or hurtful criticisms. Of course, You understand those feelings. Help us to resist taking offense and instead to consider what we can learn from the charges against us. Teach us to be still and to trust You, being slow to speak and to avoid retaliation. You are our fortress and our high tower; we are safe in Your arms. In Jesus's name, amen.*

# HEALTHY CHOICES

*Daniel resolved not to defile himself.*
DANIEL 1:8

The college experience means many things to students, but certainly one aspect of this season in life is the opportunity to make choices. It is the rare possibility to remake oneself, or at least to put oneself in the position to be remade, when a person walks onto a campus for the first time. I have also learned that the college experience means lots of free food. If the students on our campus wished to do so, they could eat one or two free meals a day, courtesy of student government and various student organizations, as these groups attempt to make themselves known to freshmen during the first two weeks of the fall semester.

The first chapter of the Old Testament book of Daniel *shares the story of four young men who had the opportunity to eat some wonderful free food as well.* Four young Jewish men, Daniel and his buddies Shadrach, Meshach, and Abednego, were taken from their homes and transplanted in Babylon after that world power had conquered Judah. In verse 8, the Scripture simply states that Daniel resolved not to defile himself. I often wonder why Daniel made that choice and how we could teach our students, experiencing some degree of stress in transition (although not to the degree of Daniel), to follow his lead in deciding to stay faithful to the Lord in a new environment. Who could blame Daniel if he were sad, depressed, and homesick? Who could blame him if he simply wanted to fit in and not make waves, learning a new language and the pagan worldview of the Babylonians? Who could blame him if he satiated his sorrow with some good food and drink? After all, I have had a cookie or ice cream plenty of times to bring comfort in the midst of emotional chaos.

But Daniel chose not to defile himself with a worldly culture, a pagan identity, and a diet that was neither healthy nor consistent with Jewish law. Was it because of his upbringing and the influence of his parents? The Bible doesn't say. Was it because he walked in an intimate and passionate relationship with the Lord? Clearly so, especially as you read the remainder of the Old Testament book named for him. Certainly, it helped that he had three friends with him who were equally committed to serving the Lord purely and with principle. That is why it is so crucial not to walk alone through life; the powerful encouragement of brothers and sisters in Christ helps me to remain faithful when temptation and adversity assault my decision to follow the Lord. There is no doubt that a battle for the minds of young people is being waged on our college campuses—and that battle is extended to the hearts and minds of all of us. Each one is being asked in myriad ways to make the decision Joshua demanded of the children of Israel in Shechem right before his death: "Choose for yourselves this day whom you will serve" (Joshua 24:15). The choice will shape the rest of their lives.

Daniel spent a long time in Babylon, nearly seven decades. He could have been angry at God or bitter over being ripped away from his home and family by the very government he was forced to serve. Instead, he exhibited his faithfulness and love for the Lord consistently through one test after another. May we all live similarly with God's help!

### PRAYER

*Heavenly Father, thank You for the grace that You extend to us when we face the round of choices that we are offered on a daily basis. While none of them seems very significant at the time, we know that they add up to a legacy that will either encourage or distract from our relationship with You. Like Daniel, we want to resolve not to defile ourselves. Instead, we want our lives to be healthy, pure, and glorifying to You. In Jesus's name, amen.*

# PRAYING THROUGH
# A PANDEMIC

*Now when Daniel learned that the decree had been published,
he went home to his upstairs room where the windows opened
toward Jerusalem. Three times a day he got down on his knees
and prayed, giving thanks to his God, just as he had done before.*

DANIEL 6:10

How does one pray in the midst of a pandemic? What should be the nature of our intercession when it feels as though the world is falling apart around us—rioting and violence in the streets, a political process poisoned by hateful partisanship and division, and willful rebellion against God at every turn? We begin by acknowledging our part in the problem. We humble ourselves, seek God's face, turn from our wicked ways—and pray that the rest of this country may do the same (2 Chronicles 7:14). Daniel found himself in a similar situation, and his prayer life is a model to emulate.

Daniel faced a crisis even worse than a pandemic in chapter six of the Old Testament book named after him. Envious bureaucrats flattered King Darius and trapped Daniel with a law prohibiting any worship other than that of the Medo-Persian monarch. The man of God faced certain death if he continued to bow down to the Lord. How did Daniel respond? Read the verse at the beginning of this devotion. First, Daniel did not try to hide his allegiance to God in the midst of the crisis; he prayed before an open window for all to see. Second, he gave thanks to God even though the circumstances were dire. And third, he simply continued to pray in the same way and with the same frequency *"as he had done before."* Daniel's devotion was so consistent that he did not have to intensify it when the heat was on. Can we apply these same principles in the present crisis? Can we offer hope to a hurting world with a sincere and visible faith? Can we find ways to thank God for His goodness and His blessings even when many doubt His existence or His love for this world? Finally, how can we cultivate a pattern of prayer now that will sustain us both on ordinary days and in extraordinary times? We want a relationship with the Lord that never needs to be adjusted, regardless of what we are facing.

The simplest prayers in a crisis are the best prayers. Faced by an attack from the Moabites and the Ammonites, King Jehoshaphat prayed, "Our God, . . . we have no power to face this vast army that is attacking us. We do not know what to do, but our eyes are on you" (2 Chronicles 20:12). When it is hard to pray, we just need to tell the Lord that: "Father, we have no power to deal with any overwhelming situation! We are just going to look to You." Even more simply, we should follow the example of Bartimaeus, the blind beggar on the road to Jericho, who, when he heard that Jesus was passing by, prayed simply, "Jesus, Son of David, have mercy on me!" (Mark 10:47) Essentially, this man needed to get God's attention and just yelled "Help!" *Pretty effective praying, too, because the Gospel writer Mark tells us that this direct, unadorned plea stopped Jesus in his tracks.*

## P R A Y E R

*Heavenly Father, 2020 has been a hard time for us and for everyone in this world. So many people are frightened and lost. People are especially vulnerable to loneliness and despair. We need You, Lord. We know that You are in control. We know that You love us more than we can imagine. Help us to be thankful and hope-filled. Use us to offer this world Your light at the end of the tunnel. Help us to pray when our minds and hearts are running in the opposite direction. In Jesus's name, amen.*

# MEETING HIM
# THROUGH PRAISE

*Enter his [God's] gates with thanksgiving and his courts
with praise; give thanks to him and praise his name.*
PSALM 100:4

Sometimes the smallest details can have the most profound significance!
As a historian as well as a pastor, I have always appreciated the meaning
of the way things are built. In my classes, I will talk to my students about
the historical importance of the construction and appearance of Gothic
cathedrals, New York City skyscrapers, Louis XIV's palace at Versailles,
London's Crystal Palace, or the buildings along the Ringstrasse in late
19th-century Vienna. No architectural detail is coincidental; we can learn
what the builders hoped to say through the way they built these historically
significant structures. The same may be said about the way that the Lord
instructed the Israelites to set up camp around the tent of meeting, the
tabernacle, during their wanderings in the wilderness on the way to the
promised land.

In Numbers 2:3, the Lord told Moses and his brother Aaron, "On the
east, toward the sunrise, the divisions of the camp of Judah are to encamp
under their standard [or banner]." The rest of the chapter lays out the
configuration for all 12 tribes to pitch their tents around the tabernacle. If
you are an insomniac, this chapter might make good reading at night—lots
of apparently tedious names and numbers to help you go to sleep (hence
the name of the book, Numbers.) But you will miss the dynamic truth that
the Lord is teaching us if you don't think about the way the Lord ordered
these tribes around the tabernacle. The tabernacle, or tent of meeting, was
exactly what its name implies, a place for the Israelites to meet God while
they were traveling through the wilderness on the way to the home the
Lord would provide for them. The cloud of God's Presence would descend
periodically on the tent of meeting, covering it and beckoning Moses,

Aaron, and the other priests to join Him in the tent to hear His instructions for His people. In order to get to the tent, you needed to proceed through the encampment of Judah, positioned right in front of the gate or entrance to the courtyard and the tabernacle.

Why is that important to know? It boils down to the meaning of the name Judah. In the Hebrew language, the name means praise. Simply put, by placing the tents of Judah right in front of the entry point to the courtyard that would lead to meeting the Presence of the Lord, God was saying to all of us that we must come to Him through praise and thanksgiving. Psalm 100, verse 4, famously asserts the same truth: "Enter his [God's] gates with thanksgiving and his courts with praise; give thanks to him and praise his name." We must begin with praise and thanksgiving as the reference point of our faith—recognizing that praise and thanksgiving are the only proper attitudes to adopt and actions to implement when we consider who God is and what He has done for us. Gratitude and worship get the "eyes of our heart" off ourselves, our worries, and our fears and put them where they belong—on Him!

Notice that in Numbers 2:3, the Lord indicates that Judah is to be camped in the direction of the sunrise. Is it a stretch, then, to encourage the act of praise in all of our lives as near to the moment of sunrise as possible each day? When we climb out of bed and our feet hit the floor, how about breathing a simple prayer of thanksgiving and praise to the Lord before we do anything else?

PRAYER

*Heavenly Father, forgive us for being so ungrateful so often in our lives. We selfishly forget Who You are, how much You love us, and all that You have done for us—starting with the Cross. Fill our minds with all that we have to be thankful for each day of our lives. We want to meet You every day we breathe in this life as we make our journey home to be with You. In Jesus's name, amen.*

# ACKNOWLEDGMENTS

There are so many people to thank without whom this book would never have been written. I'm grateful for my parents, Ben and Betsy Gates, who believed that a family should be in church, even when their oldest son found the services boring at times—and no doubt told them so on more than one occasion. After a commitment to Christ in high school, my faith was especially encouraged by my local FCA leader, John Slavich, and my "spiritual" Mom-mentor, Marti Schrader, who has believed in my ministry from those days all the way to the present.

I am grateful to all of my friends in William and Mary Christian Fellowship during my college years. It was there I received God's call to ministry, and my WMCF friends helped me to hear it and clarify that call. I am especially grateful to Larry Adams, who showed me even then how an effective campus minister could nurture student leaders and help them grow in their walk with the Lord.

The Lord taught me so much as a student at Fuller Theological Seminary in Pasadena, California, as I pursued my Master of Divinity Degree. I'm grateful for roommates and friends there whom God used to deepen and enrich my understanding of His Word and His character. Special thanks to Dr. James Bradley, who taught me not only Church History but showed me how the academic life should be approached with a heart of devotion to Jesus. I will be forever grateful for the class that I took with British pastor and church leader David Watson who taught me so much about the ministry of the Holy Spirit. And I am grateful for the years I spent attending Church on the Way in Van Nuys, California. No one taught me more about worship and a love for the Scripture than Pastor Jack Hayford.

I first learned ministry as a part of the pastoral staff of Visalia United Methodist Church in Visalia, California. I am grateful for all God taught me there through Senior Pastor Harry Wood and all of the members of that wonderful church, many of them dear friends still to this day.

While I was a history graduate student at the University of Tennessee in Knoxville, God led me to become a part of Cornerstone Church. The pastoral staff and the members of that church loved me, fed me, and strengthened my faith. Serving at Cornerstone gave me the chance to get my feet wet ministering to college students, and I am grateful for the relationships that I have with some of those students even now.

There are too many people to acknowledge who were a part of the Greater Fort Wayne Campus Ministry community from 1997–2020. Special thanks to the students I coached and mentored—you will always be my "CM kids." I'm grateful for the support of all of those people who believed in the significance of what we were doing on campus and contributed time, energy, and resources to the success of the ministry.

I'm grateful to Tim Beals, President of Credo Communications, for guiding me and encouraging me through the publication process. Thanks to Janet Gates, Wink and Marcia Litton, Joe Clark, Kent Kauffman, Nigel James, Gary Smith, Marti Schrader, Marvin Bozard, Randy Dodd, and Fred Stayton for their willingness to look over early drafts of this book and make helpful suggestions.

I am grateful that the Lord gave me the best two sons that I could have ever asked for in Alex and Benjamin. They have taught me so much, and I love them dearly. The Lord gave Alex and our whole family a terrific gift when he married Morgan; I'm grateful for her and her encouragement.

Most of all, I am thankful for my wife, Janet. God has used her to show me His love and to teach me so much. She is my best friend and the best partner a man could ask for. She is God's gift to me.

# ABOUT THE AUTHOR

**Dr. Ben Gates** served as the Executive Director of Greater Fort Wayne Campus Ministry and a campus pastor at (Indiana University) Purdue University Fort Wayne and the Indiana Institute of Technology from 1997–2020. He continues to teach as a Senior Lecturer with the Purdue University Fort Wayne Department of History and has been a member of that Department since 1997. Dr. Gates earned a Master of Divinity Degree from Fuller Theological Seminary in Pasadena, California, and an MA and PhD in history from the University of Tennessee in Knoxville. As a campus minister, he has trained hundreds of student leaders, as well as several campus ministry interns. During these years, he led 26 cross-cultural mission trips to 11 countries on three continents, building a network of international ministry partners. Ben and his wife, Janet, an elementary school teacher, have been married for 23 years. Their family includes two grown sons, Alex and Benjamin; Alex's wife, Morgan; their sweet but eccentric Shichon, Keelie; and their grand-dog, Gus Gus.

Dr. Gates is available to speak at conferences, camps, or retreats. He is also prepared to lead mission trips for interested groups. He may be contacted at *AWordThatSustains@gmail.com*.